# Being And Becoming Excellent - Reflections

*Charles O. Barker, M.D.*

Being And Becoming Excellent - Reflections

Copyright © 2023 Charles Barker
All rights reserved. ISBN: 978-1-915911-47-6
Printed in the United States of America.

No part of this publication shall be reproduced, transmitted, or sold in whole or in part in any form without prior written consent of the author, except as provided by the United States of America copyright law. Any unauthorized usage of the text without express written permission of the publisher is a violation of the author's copyright and is illegal and punishable by law. All trademarks and registered trademarks appearing in this guide are the property of their respective owners.

For permission requests, write to the publisher, addressed "Attention: Permissions Coordinator," at the address below.

Amazon Book Publishing Center, 420 Terry Ave N, Seattle, Washington, 98109, U.S.A

The opinions expressed by the Author are not necessarily those held by Amazon Book Publishing Center.

Ordering Information: Quantity sales and special discounts are available on quantity purchases by corporations, associations, and others. For details, contact the publisher at info@amazonbookpublishingcenter.com.

The information contained within this book is strictly for informational purposes. The material may include information, products, or services by third parties. As such, the Author and Publisher do not assume responsibility or liability for any third-party material or opinions. The publisher is not responsible for websites (or their content) that are not owned by the publisher. Readers are advised to do their own due diligence when it comes to making decisions.

Amazon Book Publishing Center works with authors, and aspiring authors, who have a story to tell and a brand to build. Do you have a book idea you would like us to consider publishing? Please visit AmazonBookPublishingCenter.com for more information.

# DEDICATION

To my beloved wife of fifty-plus years Conoly Lemon Barker, to my "three jewels"—Emma Suzanne McDonald, Thomas Harrison Barker, and Lucy Anne Barker Durbin, to Sean McDonald, Shannon Doyle Barker, Shane Durbin, and Jonathan Casimir who was son-in-law for a while, to my grandchildren—Joshua Paul McDonald, Kyle Ashton and Manda Monk Casimir, Aidan Thomas Casimir, Benny Durbin, Finn Doyle Barker, and my "namesake," Leo Charles Barker. God has blessed me richly through my family!

Being And Becoming Excellent - Reflections

*Whatever is true, whatever is honorable, whatever is just, whatever is pure, whatever is pleasing, whatever is commendable, if there is any excellence and if there is anything worthy of praise, think about these things. —Paul of Tarsus, c. 55 CE[1]*

[1] *Unless otherwise stated, all Christian biblical citations are from New Revised Standard Version, 1989*

## Table of Contents

DEDICATION ..................................................................................... 3

PREFACE ........................................................................................... 7

FOREWORD ...................................................................................... 9

PROLOGUE ..................................................................................... 13

    A NOT-SO-SHORT NOTE ABOUT LANGUAGE ............................................. 15

    THE HIGGS BOSON PARTICLE ................................................................ 20

INTRODUCTION .............................................................................. 23

REFLECTION 1—REFLECTIONS ON OUR ORIGINS/TRADITIONS ........... 29

REFLECTION 2—OUR TRUE NATURE ................................................ 37

REFLECTION 3—ON MORALITY AND ETHICS .................................... 51

REFLECTION 4—RELATIONALITY/RESPONSIBILITY ETHICS ............... 61

REFLECTION 5—APPLICATION OF THE "NEW" ETHIC ....................... 68

    CT REFLECTS ON A FAMILY MEDICINE ROTATION EXPERIENCE .................. 68

    SP'S REFLECTION ................................................................................. 71

    JW'S REFLECTION ............................................................................... 74

REFLECTION 6—LOVE AND COMPASSION ........................................ 80

    LOVE .................................................................................................. 80

    COMPASSION ..................................................................................... 85

REFLECTION 7—FORGIVENESS, RECONCILIATION, AND RESTORATION ................................................................................. 91

REFLECTION 8—THE PATH TO TRUE PEACE AND HEALING .............. 97

| | |
|---|---|
| THE MOST EXCELLENT WAY | 97 |
| THE CHARTER FOR COMPASSION | 97 |
| **END NOTES** | **102** |
| **EPILOGUE** | **115** |
| **ACKNOWLEDGEMENTS** | **117** |
| **BIBLIOGRAPHY** | **120** |

# Preface

    This is my story, an autobiography. In a way, I suppose I am the audience. However, I would like to think the general reader, such as my own family and friends, as well as their families and friends might be interested in this story. Anyone seeking a more excellent way of life might be interested. And those interested in life after this physical life may enjoy the section on "supersymmetry."

I have striven toward excellence my entire life, seeking in my youth to be simply a "good guy." So, there may be some wisdom and practices herein that will appeal. The stories and reflections are multilevel. Most reflections begin with a personal story. This is followed by a "deeper" scientific, philosophic story that for me explains the who, when, what, how, and why. One thing I have discovered and know to be true: humans everywhere share a common humanity and are interdependent. We have common needs and individual special needs, also special gifts to offer. So, we ought to embrace and appreciate diversity and respect each other, supporting each other with love and compassion. My story makes a case for these fundamental truths.

I have lived a relatively long life, filled with many blessings and many personal losses and sufferings. With these personal stories and deeper reflections, there is much to think about and ponder. If you are a general reader, perhaps just reading the stories at the beginning of each reflection and spending time with the last few reflections would be fruitful for you. These latter reflections give some guidance on praxis (practice) on how to become more excellent and more compassionate, which is so needed in today's world.

If you are a lover and reader of science, religion, or philosophy, you may find the deeper reflections, along with the endnotes, interesting, thought-provoking, and enlightening. Take what appeals and leave what does not.

If your reflections lead to a desire to become more excellent, more loving, more compassionate, and to take specific, positive actions toward these ends, then my story will have accomplished its intended purpose.

- *C.O. Barker, M.D.*

# FOREWORD

The title of Dr. Barker's book, I think, tells us what it is about, but more importantly it defines for me and as you read hopefully for you, what is the human experience with its various possibilities of living, and that the reality in which we live, the universe, is ever moving, in flux, and so is our interaction with it. We are warned that this work will be encompassing, perhaps demanding, and certainly illuminating. The "Being" in the title reminds us that humans are living beings; our very nature is one of life and death. What we do as this being brings us to the next part of the title, "Becoming Excellent." We all are, but to become excellent, Dr. Barker tells us, is a choice that we make. It involves understanding ourselves and having an awareness of the world around us that forms the context in which we live. His work tackles the question of how we know who we are and who we are becoming as individuals, as communities, and as a world population, and concludes with a discussion of a practical universal ethic relevant to the 21st century.

The last part of the title, "Reflections," tells us how he will wrestle with the questions of life, our being and becoming as creatures in this universe. Dr. Barker willingly shares his life experiences as a place to begin our study. He reflects on his personal experiences in the context of scientific, philosophical, and theological thinkers through the ages, molding a picture of humanity's commonality which preserves paradoxically our individuality. Reflecting as a way of becoming more excellent as life progresses has guided Dr. Barker and he shares his way. By his sharing of the personal we are encouraged to remember, reflect, and share, a process that can make us more aware of both our common humanity and our communal and individual differences, which can enable us to choose to live in peace and justice worldwide.

Dr. Barker begins by discussing the limiting nature of language. Different cultures, disciplines, socioeconomic classes, nationalities, all have their own language, their own "truth" and methodology for determining it, their own beliefs, their own way of viewing the world; these differences make communication tainted unless we are willing as Dr. Barker suggests to open up, step outside ourselves, risk seeing other possibilities, and search for a greater truth. I find these reflections show us a way to cross boundaries, find deeper connections, and choose more humanely.

Of particular concern to Dr. Barker is the dialogue between the disciplines of science and religion, a dialogue that once was considered impossible. Most assert that the two disciplines approach the basic questions of the universe and life from different perspectives, each valid within their sphere, but Dr. Barker asks us to delve deeper, and find in the different expressions a statement nearer to the Truth. He sees in the modern scientists' theory of supersymmetry a suggestion of life beyond this life. He has pondered the connection, still only theoretical, between the physicists' Standard Model which defines the basics of our symmetric universe and the idea of supersymmetry which theoretically balances and fills in the gaps in the model; he wonders if the connection between the two can be Kierkegaard's idea of faith. He sees an interconnectivity between physical reality and spiritual reality, the physical we know, dependent on a spiritual we only see in part. Perhaps science and religion can affirm each other, a conversation worth having, I think. Dr. Barker certainly opens that door.

Dr. Barker suggests that you, the reader, can skip the first four reflections and go straight to the practical applications of determining right action now is your concern, but I recommend you don't. Yes, the early reflections are more involved intellectually, drawing on the works of scientists, philosophers, and theologians throughout human history, but they build a rationale for the practical ethical model he presents in the later reflections. He describes first how humans have evolved into conscious being; then he discusses who we are from a biological developmental perspective placing us in an increasingly known reality contained in even greater spirituality reality. After discussing the various ethical systems proposed by philosophers and theologians in the past, Dr. Barker suggests in our time we need a universal ethical system based on being and becoming. Expanding on Charles Curran's Relationship-Responsibility model Dr. Barker develops an ethic based on the core values of love and compassion, the reality that we hurt each other, and that we can learn to live compassionately. We have a choice he asserts; at this point I have a conviction that the spiritual realm has a greater impact on our choosing of which we are mostly unaware until we have crossed the boundary of deciding; nevertheless, we choose. Others may question some of his conclusions, interpretations, and assumptions presented, but that is part of what Dr. Barker wants—an open, real, personal, and general conversation that moves from theory to practical, from personal to philosophical, from thought to action. These parts of his work help us act within a more global context, understand why our values differ from those in other communities, and understand the philosophical, scientific, and theological bases that underpin what we and others do. I find that these reflections push me to a deeper place from which to decide and in which there is a connection with all.

Dr. Barker's ultimate purpose is to propose a practical ethical system, one based in a more excellent way, one that is restorative of community, and one that can be taught. The last reflections offer specific suggestions for how we can learn to live more compassionately, learn to forgive, reconcile, and restore. Specific examples from Dr. Barker's experience form a picture of how the framework of a relationality-responsibility ethic can work in practice. Both success and failure can be clearly seen and the difficult and twisted path one must walk to respond within this ethical system. Intentionality, awareness, courage and hard work necessarily are a part of 21$^{st}$ century ethics. Dr. Barker's work with the International Charter for Compassion gave him a concrete experience in the validity of this work and its value in bringing the world to a just and lasting peace.

I have known Charlie since he came to Dallas to retire. We had a connection since my daughter lives in Honolulu which was the last posting of his naval career. Our conversations deepened as he earned his degree at Perkins Theological Seminary. We have continued now on a regular basis meeting to talk about life, science, theology, and the practical concerns of living. This work is a true reflection of who he is, the wisdom gained through reflection on personal experiences and the ideas of scientists and theologians, a wisdom he has used to guide his life of action. His reflections suggest we too can choose to reflect on the life we live consciously and constantly within the context of our experience, the experience of those around us, and the works of thinkers through the ages, a process that can lead to a more excellent being. The wisdom shared in this book is well worth the readers time and consideration and I am thankful Charlie is sharing it with us.

-*Caroline Martin*

*March 14, 2023*

# Prologue

*Post WWII, 1952: I was six or seven years old. It seemed that all adults smoked cigarettes. And there I sat on a stool, facing the corner of the bedroom. "Just you sit there until your dad gets home, and don't you move," my momma said gently, but with a firmness that meant business. So, there I sat anxious, miserable, bored, and fearful of what my dad was going to do to me when he got home.*

*I had a secret. My momma would open her pocketbook, take out a package of cigarettes, tap one out, and put the filtered end in her mouth. Cigarettes were filtered, by then. Momma would light her cigarette and take a nice, long draw, turning her head slightly and blowing the smoke upwards, to avoid blowing directly into someone's face. Then she would put the pack of cigarettes along with the lighter back into her pocketbook. I thought it was neat, so adult-like. My daddy smoked, too. I must have been raised in a room full of smoke. Ashtrays were in every room. Our old dining room table had cigarette burns at the edges where Momma or Daddy or some friend would lay a cigarette down briefly. (I inherited this family heirloom table. It sits in our dining room today, refinished, with cigarette burns and all.)*

*Anyway, to me, being a grownup meant being able to smoke cigarettes—my momma and daddy showed me that. One day, when Momma was out of the room and away from her pocketbook, I took some of her cigarettes and hid them in the garage, which was separate from the house. I had one of those giveaway booklets of matches, which I had hidden in the garage, as well. When I went out to play, I'd go into the garage and pretend to smoke a cigarette: I'd light it up, and put it between my lips, but I never was quite able to inhale like Momma. I felt so adult! So very neat...I felt "grown-up."*

*Two sisters lived down the street from us, one about my age and one younger. My sister Anne and I played with them. They lived in a nicer house and, obviously, had more toys, nicer clothes, and overall* were spoiled, at least to my thinking. One day, my sister wasn't there when we were playing, and, out of the blue, I said to Melanie (not her real name) who was my age, "Guess what? I have a secret." Melanie, of course, wanted to know what it was, insisted, and because I thought it was so neat, I told her about my cigarettes in the garage.

Mistake! That very same day Melanie told my sister, who promptly tattled on me. So, I found myself confronting Momma who, of course, referred the matter to my daddy, who would take care of things when he came home from work. When he came into the bedroom, which was connected to the bathroom, he said, "Son, let's go into the bathroom." Oh, dreaded time, here, now—I had no words—caught red-handed since Momma had retrieved the stolen cigarettes and matches from the garage. Daddy already knew the story.

As we walked into the bathroom, he directed me to sit on the toilet seat. He pulled out his belt, held it in his hand, and then squatted down in front of me. He said, "Son, this is not all your fault. Your mother and I are equally responsible. You see us smoking cigarettes all the time, which is not good. We have not been good examples. You are not to ever do this again. When you get much older you can decide for yourself. Until then, I expect you not to do this. Do you understand?" Oh, precious relief, "Yes, sir!" I responded. Daddy then put his arm around me, and we walked out of the bathroom together. I never smoked again, at least until my college years.

There is an epitaph on Daddy and Momma's memorial headstone at the cemetery in Valdosta, Georgia. It reads, "They taught us the true meaning of 'I love you.'" The cigarette story is just one of many stories about my parents that give testimony to the truth of that epitaph. The headstone has engraved on it the first names of our siblings in order of birth: Ashley, Freddie, Anne, Charles, and Warren. I think about that memorial stone today, remember the cigarette story, and think of my daddy's love and compassion for me and the way he expressed it.

This story tells of one of my earliest childhood experiences. Obviously, the memory has stuck in my mind, and the recollection is as if it "just happened." Throughout my life, I have experienced a lot, read a lot, acquired a lot of knowledge and credentials, and reflected a great deal on my life and life in general. I am convinced that our physical, emotional, intellectual, and spiritual nature is a complex mixture of potential and possibilities for both good and bad. I believe we are self-centered, likely due to our instinct to survive, but we also have the potential and are hardwired neurologically for kindness, empathy, and compassion. This book reflects my journey to become less self-centered and more other-centered, more loving, and compassionate.

I have found that using the "expanded Golden Rule" as a guiding principle from moment to moment is key. The Golden Rule inspires us to treat others as we wish to be treated and not to treat others as we would not wish to be treated. Expanded, the rule means to treat others as they wish to be treated and not treat others as they would wish not to be treated. This is impossible to do unless we get to know others and develop a good relationship with them. How can I treat another person by how they wish to be treated or not treated if I do not really know them? So, herein are a few of my life experiences in getting to know the other. But first…

### *A not-so-short note about language*

I have come to be comfortable with languages, even those I do not really understand. I am open to learning all languages because I am convinced that each contains great wisdom and truth, both universal and common. I am equally convinced that though each language expresses a part of the truth, we can only know the truth more fully by being open to all languages of expression. For me, language is the expression of an entity's state of being in motion, its needs, desires, knowledge, feelings, experiential stories, and consciousness. It may be verbal or non-verbal, be animate (living) or inanimate (non-living). Understanding language matures over time if we are open. If I am open and listen intentionally, moment by moment, to self, to others, and to the environment, I can hear the joy, pain, and suffering of any entity: my fellow human beings, the environment organic and inorganic, and even myself. The language may be expressed in the simple, everyday secular terminology of a national language or local dialect; or it may be in religious or scientific terms; it may be in the terminology expressed directly by simply being earth, sun, moon, stars, and cosmos, all in motion along what theoretical physicists call the arrow of time.

Regardless of the language expressed—political, sociocultural, religious, or scientific—I sense that truth as we can know it is ultimately limited; however, each expression points to a greater truth. How we discover truth differs by the methodology we use. Whether the methodology is political and ideological, spiritual/religious/interfaith, or scientific, each method or process is quite powerful in its way of describing truth. It points to a more universal, cosmic truth. In the Christian religious tradition, Jesus is attributed with the saying, "I still have many things to say to you, but you cannot bear them now. When the Spirit of truth comes, he will guide you into all the truth."[2] For me, "all truth" means ALL truth, not just a small bit of truth, and that requires "opening up" with an inquiring mind to the possibilities and probabilities. That can be scary, but also quite wonderful and joyful. It requires us to step outside ourselves and look, see, and come along on a wild ride that reveals greater and greater truth.

Everyone has a social location with their language or languages. Mine is unique, as is yours. I was born in southern Georgia in 1945, just as World War II ended, at a time when the Civil Rights Movement was yet to be and when segregation of Negro black and Caucasian white was the accepted norm. I grew up learning and using the English language. The religious language and terminology of the area were primarily Christian, and that is what I learned; diverse religious language was not to be heard in the local culture. Knowledge and experience of other religious languages were not necessary, given the place and time. Each religion had its location and community, and "ne'er the twain shall meet." I was raised in the Judeo-Christian Protestant tradition, first with Disciples of Christ, later with Southern Baptist, and even later with Presbyterian Church (USA), which I currently embrace. I knew some of my schoolmates and next-door neighbor friends were of other religious traditions and language, but that did not matter to us as children in our day-to-day play with each other, since there was no "religious talk" per se. I vividly remember the adage, "If you want to keep a friendship, you don't talk politics or religion."

Today, in our shrinking world with its rapid transportation systems and instantaneous communications, not talking politics and religion—and science—has changed for me, as I suspect it has changed for many reading this book. If there is to be any true peace and healing of this world and its suffering humanity and environment, then each of us must learn as many languages as possible and be open and willing to dialogue across them.

I became interested in math and science early. Through a passion for entomology, zoology, and astronomy, I learned those languages and used the knowledge unabashedly to catch many a butterfly, dissect many a backyard frog, and photograph the multiple phases of a lunar eclipse in 1959 for a high school science project. An interest in genetics led serendipitously to a science project on cancer in mice in 1962 when I won first place in the region and third place in a state competition. I went on to receive a Bachelor of Arts in Chemistry, and later, a Doctor of Medicine degree at Emory University, Atlanta.

I learned the languages of math and science, biology, chemistry, and physics. Those languages were integral to the artful language of medicine, a language that became primary for me as a family physician in southern Georgia. Enjoying clinical practice as a family doctor for many years, I treated individuals of religious and non-religious persuasions, nurturing close relationships, and thereby learning the religious and non-religious languages of many. Regardless of the language, fundamentally, I discovered that each of us has the same basic needs and a desire to flourish for self and family and that each of us experiences joy, happiness, suffering, and eventual death. More important, I learned to put myself in the shoes of my patients, to truly respect them in the context of family and community, and to show compassion and love. Many times, that meant using the language of tough love!

Desert Shield/Desert Storm came along in 1990, and I re-entered naval medical service a second time, having previously served from 1972 to

1975 during the Vietnam War. At the end of Desert Shield/Desert Storm in 1991 I remained in military medicine and became an Aerospace Medicine specialist, learning yet another language. Over the ensuing seventeen-year military medicine career, my wife and I encountered the languages of many other cultures and religions as we frequently changed locations. I retired in 2007.

On a lighter note, upon retirement, I proposed to my wife that we stay in Hawaii, where we were living at the time. After all, it is paradise, right? She said, "Well, if you want to live with me you are going to Dallas, Texas!" Dallas is where our two daughters and three grandsons lived. Well, not much argument...here I am in Dallas. And, in retrospect, I consider that move a real blessing.

I must admit that I have flourished in Dallas. Using the familiar language of Christianity, I felt a "call" in late 2009 to study theology in-depth. So, in the fall of 2010, I entered Southern Methodist University Perkins School of Theology, attending part-time, and completed a Master of Theological Studies in the spring of 2014. I felt that I already had the greatest advisor/guide/ spiritual director anyone could have —the Holy Spirit— even before entering Perkins. So, when one of my conservative Christian friends admonished me at the beginning of my studies, "Why would you want to spend good money to go to a place like Perkins (a fairly liberal seminary)," I quipped, "Well, maybe Perkins needs me as much as I need Perkins."

In retrospect, having had many subsequent theological discussions with my conservative and liberal Christian friends and my non-religious friends, I think all would agree that my decision to complete the course of study and learn yet another language was a good one. Over the years, we have enjoyed great dialogues across many divides and are still friends!

I remember one such dialogue with my conservative Christian friends when the topic of America as a Christian nation came up. A few commented that our nation had been founded as a Christian nation since the way of life of its earliest New World settlers had been inherited from Old World western Europe. Some in our group lamented that we have lost who we were as a nation and that other religions are taking over. I reminded my friends that I, along with many others of all religious persuasions, fought for this nation, a nation founded on the principle of freedom of religion, that each person has the freedom to worship in her or his own way if it doesn't hurt the others. My friends' responses were each some variation of the statement, "Oh, yes, of course, that's right." We are still friends.

More important, learning a broader, more in-depth theological/religious language has opened me to many faith traditions in the Dallas-Fort Worth area. This has led to deeper relationships through presence and dialogue as I made new friends with Buddhists, Hindus, Baha'i, Jews, Muslims, and with Christians of all denominations. Within the interfaith community, there are those professing no religious faith at all with whom I have also become friends. I keep rediscovering the bottom-line truth: our common humanity. We all have the same basic needs, including the desire to flourish for ourselves, our families, and our relationships with others. Each of us experiences joy, happiness, suffering, and eventual death. And as responsible stewards of our environment, we all are called to love and have compassion for mother earth. We should be convinced, based on what we currently know and have experienced, that continued human existence on earth depends on love and compassion, forgiveness, reconciliation, and restoration of our environment. Our indigenous communities have much to offer in this process.

Finally, along with experiencing multiple religious languages and new-found friends, I continue to be amazed at the language of science, especially physics, and chemistry, although I am a biologist at heart. How might we look at the current language of the cosmos, our knowledge of it, and see how the language of science and the language of religion might be saying the same things about ultimate truths, about bottom-line realities?

Being And Becoming Excellent - Reflections

### *The Higgs Boson Particle*

Bear with me here for the language of physics. For years, theoretical particle physicists, such as Peter Higgs, have postulated a quantum field with its associated particle, the Higgs Boson, from which all physical matter—you, me, my coffee cup— everything is made. In October 1999, one physicist described the Higgs Boson in Scientific American:

> "Over the past few decades, particle physicists have developed an elegant theoretical model (the Standard Model) that gives a framework for our current understanding of the fundamental particles and forces of nature. One major ingredient in this model is a hypothetical, ubiquitous quantum field that is supposed to be responsible for giving particles their masses (this field would answer the basic question of why particles have the masses they do—or indeed, why they have any masses at all). This field is called the Higgs field. Because of wave-particle duality, all quantum fields have a fundamental particle associated with them. The particle associated with the Higgs field is called the Higgs boson.
>
> "Because the Higgs field would be responsible for mass, the very fact that the fundamental particles do have mass is regarded by many physicists as an indication of the existence of the Higgs field. We can even take all our data on particle physics

and interpret them in terms of the mass of a hypothetical Higgs boson. In other words, if we assume that the Higgs boson exists, we can infer its mass based on the effect it would have on the properties of other particles and fields. We have not yet truly proved that the Higgs boson exists, however. One of the main aims of particle physics over the next couple of decades is to prove once and for all the existence or nonexistence of the Higgs boson."[3]

Fast forward thirteen years. On July 4, 2012, the Higgs Boson particle, and therefore the Higgs field, were proven, thanks to the effort of over three thousand physicists worldwide and the Large Hadron Collider (LHC) at Europe's particle-physics laboratory, CERN, near Geneva, Switzerland. On that date, a particle with 125 GeV mass/energy was detected, thus proving what was postulated decades earlier, a particle that quickly appeared and then quickly disappeared. Physicists were ecstatic. The significance of this discovery cannot be overstated. As expressed by theoretical physicist Sean Carroll, and I paraphrase: With the discovery of the Boson particle and with the reality of the Higgs field, which completes the standard model of symmetry, we can pretty much explain all physical phenomena.[4]

Along with other theoretical physicists, Carroll postulated in his 2012 book *The Particle at the End of the Universe,* that all these data seem to point to a supersymmetry principle connecting all the elements of the well-defined standard symmetrical model. Currently, there is no evidence for this supersymmetry. More on this later, and more to the point here: Might this language of physics have a comparative religious language? For example, regarding human consciousness: What is "consciousness" from a physical as well as a religious/spiritual perspective? In his 2014 TED Talk, philosopher David Chalmers posed the "hard problem" or question: What and Why is consciousness?[5] He answers by describing what he thought others might consider a crazy idea: Perhaps consciousness is as fundamental to physical reality as are electrons, protons, neutrons, atoms, and molecules. If so, then at some point, we should be able to detect, measure, and define its characteristics. He admitted we know little from a neuroscience perspective. He mentioned the insightful research of neuroscientist Giulio Tononi on the higher level of human consciousness and the "Phi measure," as compared with lower levels of consciousness. The implication of Chalmers' self-described crazy idea is that there exists some amount of consciousness at every level of matter, beginning with the earliest post-Big Bang particles/quantum wave forms to first molecules, evolving from complex inorganic substances to earliest life forms, earliest hominid forms, to our own Homo Sapien, human, self-aware, conscious brain. Admittedly, a final solution to the "hard problem" of consciousness does not currently exist. The same can be said of proof of the idea of a supersymmetry principle. Proof does not exist. But both ideas are wildly exciting to think about. Does supersymmetry give us a glimpse of the reality after life? Are we getting closer to understanding all truth?

From the perspective of language, might the religious, spiritual language of "let the indwelling Holy Spirit be your guide" be similar to the secular language of "let your conscience be your guide?" Both suggest an internal truth that reflects on itself, regulating, checking, guiding, even directing, and encouraging movement from one natural state of being to another. Does this perhaps lead us to a more excellent state of being? Parenthetically, we have no fully developed language to describe what we know and what we do not know about consciousness. However, the language is developing.

One of the underlying purposes of this book is to suggest the need for openness to a unifying language of science and spirituality. Such openness should motivate us to compare and connect different language terminologies, phrases, ideas, and definitions in a meaningful way. I have a sense, as do many, that there is a spiritual reality within every physical reality. Throughout these reflections, we will attempt to illustrate the interconnectivity, yet dependence, of physical reality upon spiritual reality, or, if rephrased based on our understanding from theoretical physics, symmetry's interconnectivity with supersymmetry, yet dependence upon supersymmetry for its existence. A paradox: separate, yet inseparable.

Charles O. Barker, M.D

# Introduction

I was born; I am becoming. You were born, and wherever you are in space and time, you are a special, unique, living, complex organism. Even as you read these words, you are becoming. The question for me and you is: Who am I, and who will I become?" Each of us is unique and made of wonderful "stardust,"[6] and each of us constitutes one in a community of human beings; of animal and plant life; of air, water, and fire; of rock and soil; of sun and moon; of planet and cosmos, here and now. We have come a long way from our beginnings—at least to the extent that we have come to know of our beginnings. From the Big Bang, from the first atoms, elements, molecules, and life, we have become a world of complex forms most beautiful, both living and nonliving. And we are still becoming and will continue to become. Still, the question persists: who will I become, who will you become, and who will we become as a living community on this planet in this cosmos?

This story is about you and me and the global community, who we are by nature, and who and how we may likely become in the future. We do have agency and choice to one degree or another. We are a collective of individuals, a community striving together, choosing goodness with the aim of being the best we can be, choosing to become excellent, or choosing badness. It is a story of how we might achieve goodness, true peace, and healing as a community by a better understanding of our nature and our personal and communal past, and by intentionally choosing a better way of becoming and relating morally and ethically toward each other and the earth. The bottom line for me: I believe who we become, as individuals and as a community, is primarily a matter of individual and collective choice and will. This choice to become excellent and to do "right" and make things "right" begins with you and with me. It begins where we are, here and now.

My story and your story begin with love—an erotic, biologic, libido kind of love. This kind of love is the most compelling and the most physically intimate. It connects one human being with another, an egg from one joining the sperm of another. About nine months later, the miracle that is you and the miracle that is me came into this world: your birthday, my birthday. Some say each of us is born as a blank slate. Others say, no, that each of us already has certain genetic tendencies and predispositions that have been passed on through previous generations and are expressed by you and me. Both opinions are true at some level, but regardless, immediately after birth, you and I have common, special needs: food, clothing, shelter, and security. And for normal development, each of us has a definite need for another's human presence, for loving touch that fills our need for security. All these needs must be filled for our optimum development physically, mentally, emotionally, and spiritually. When these basic needs are met adequately, our minds and our consciousness are likely to develop and project normally, perhaps even flourish. You and I are born with great potential to be/to become good or not so good, and at extremes, to be/to become a saint or a demon. The choices made for us early in life and the choices you and I make later in life depend much on the environment into which each of us was born and on the situations in which we develop and grow. We grow physically and develop mentally, emotionally, and spiritually. But who I am now is not who I was, and it does not necessarily determine who I will become in the long term; neither will you be in the future the person you are now. The arrow of time does not allow us to remain the same even from moment to moment. Therein lies our hope and joy, and our suffering, despair, and tragedy. Indeed, the condition in which we find ourselves today depends on the accumulation of choices we made in the past and on the circumstances within which we find ourselves. You and I can choose Paul of Tarsus' idea of excellence or not. The reality is that each of us, regardless of our choices, will experience joy, pain, and suffering during our life's journey. We hope that we can deal with the pain and suffering with equanimity, and perhaps even with a degree of joy. Is that possible? I think so.

This book is about developing a life of excellence through a state of being that leads to contentment and peace in relationship to yourself, to others, to the community, to the environment, and to the world around us.

Reflection 1 focuses on our very beginnings: our creation and our becoming aware of ourselves and our surroundings, and my attempt to explain it. It is a brief, but broad overview of our earliest origins, citing some of the Nobel prize-winning work of biologist Jacque Monod, a World War II underground Frenchman activist. We also glean wisdom from Monod's good friend, Albert Camus, another French Nobel Prize-winner who chose life over suicide. We discover British author Karen Armstrong, TED Prize winner, founder of the Charter for Compassion, and historical researcher-writer who focuses on our tribal beginnings and early spiritual and religious development, both good and bad. I present a quick summary of the ancient religious traditions, of Axial-Age giants Gautama Siddhartha, Confucius, and the philosophies of Socrates, Plato, and Aristotle, all of whom contributed significantly to what we today consider excellence. Though many today do not accept "religion" in the traditional sense of the word, many recognize and accept our inherently human "spiritual" nature, and they do not deny the positive contributions made by the world's religions to our common understanding of universal morality and values, which drive our ethical behavior today.

Reflection 2 focuses on our human nature from an evolutionary and developmental perspective. The reflection considers important ideas about the meaning of life and our basic needs and desires. The reality of death and our unconscious denial of it explains our need for security and acceptance. It explains the phenomenon of psychological transference, best described and illustrated by cultural anthropologist Ernest Becker in his 1973 classic *"Denial of Death"*.

You and I have the potential to be good and bad and everything in between. From a biological perspective, it appears we each fall somewhere on that ubiquitous Bell-shaped curve or three-dimensional cone. As individuals, we find ourselves somewhere among the combinations and permutations of goodness-badness, oscillating constantly as we make choices along the arrow of time. The potential is great, and there are those along our journey who can help us make optimal choices that lead to more joy and less suffering. (As a side note, by what criteria do we decide what is good or bad or evil? This is where the religious and ethical traditions of the world have been and continue to be helpful).

Reflection 3 presents the major moral and ethical theories and principles of the 18th and 19th centuries of the Common Era (CE), which have become integral to our social and cultural morality and ethics today. Immanuel Kant, Jeremy Bentham, and John Stuart Mill made significant, positive contributions to our understanding of moral and ethical life. Many ethicists today believe these theories fall short of our need for a more meaningful and practical ethical system. They propose a theory that considers not only the well-recognized universal moral principles and norms but also the dynamic nature of our personal and communal relationships in a complex global community. What is needed is what I would call an ontological theory, i.e., basically, a theory of being.

Reflection 4 addresses this ontological theory, citing some of the work of Christian theologian-ethicists Richard Niebuhr and Charles Curran, work which led Curran to describe a "relationality-responsibility model."[7] Although his description of the model is confined to Catholic moral tradition, I have decontextualized and applied the model to a more universal context, using a "blank-slate" thought experiment. In essence, a person comes into a conscious relationship with self, with others, and with community/society and the environment. To realize more excellent relationships of mutual respect, harmony, peace, and less suffering, we must make moment-by-moment responsible choices in thoughts, words, and actions. Within this reflection, I present the method of kenosis, i.e., the "emptying" or "negating" of oneself, which opens the way for many possibilities. For me, kenosis has promise as a method for bridging differences in language, polarities, and gaps, thereby increasing the potential for good, responsible relationships filled with deep understanding.

In Reflection 5, I apply this ethical model to the biomedical arena. The model can be applied to any sector of life—political, economic, social, religious, and environmental. As I have noted, Charles Curran originally described the Relationality-Responsibility Model, which he applied specifically to the Catholic Church. In *The Catholic Moral Tradition Today*

(1999), Curran explains his concept of a relationality-responsibility ethic. Therein, he attempts to increase Catholic awareness and understanding of what he sees is a major disconnect. On the one hand, the Church has become more sensitive to individual, personal conscience, morality, and ethics. On the other hand, the Church is hierarchical and slow to yield from its dogmatic and doctrinal ethics. Curran hopes that the Church will move toward a more sensitive relationality-responsibility ethic and away from the rigid ethics of the past. Because I am most experienced in the art and science of medicine, I will use the field of medicine to illustrate and reflect on the major principles of this new ethic.

A relatively long life of experience has taught me that there can be no true healing or peace without love and compassion and true respect for others. This is especially true when differing languages and expressions of culture, ethnicity, science, religion, economics, and politics are considered. Many wrongs have been committed in the name of each language. Without being open to other languages, having a sense of wonder, and being willing to forgive, reconcile, and restore, there can be no real healing of broken individual, community, national, or global relationships. Reflections 6 through 8 reflect deeply on these core values and ethical principles, and they also emphasize that practice is basic to our achieving optimal, more excellent, responsible relationships.

Reflection 6 describes what we mean by love and compassion. Theologian Paul Tillich argues that agape love is supreme to all other ideas of love, but all forms are innate and integral to every human being. The English term "love" is certainly complex, as I will describe. If love is on one side of the coin, then I believe compassion is on the other side. The value of compassion resides at the very core of every world religion and spiritual tradition, each espousing a variant of the Golden Rule as its primary guiding principle. I argue that the two core values of love and compassion are essential to an excellent way of life. When these qualities are cultivated intentionally and operationally from the beginning of human life, love and compassion develop harmonious, responsible relationships with unity in thought, word, and deed among individuals, families, communities, nations, and the world. The question then becomes, "How do I/we become more loving and compassionate?"

In Reflection 7, I shift gears to come face-to-face with reality: We hurt ourselves, we hurt others, and we hurt the environment. Perfect examples of this are plentiful. Just look around. Turn on the media and see what's happening every day. This is the existential fact that prevents or disrupts the unity, joy, peace, and harmony we humans and the world desperately need. To move from this existential fact to one that supports others and seeks their flourishing, we must cultivate the values of compassion and compassionate action. I spend some time reflecting on the South African experience of apartheid as an example of the kind of process necessary to move toward peace and healing.

Reflection 8 describes how we can learn, embody, and live in this exceptional way; how we can be more compassionate to self, to others, and within systems; how we can forgive and be more grateful, both key to a compassionate life. The section emphasizes understanding our common humanity, that we are all interconnected and interdependent. Finally, I reflect on several compassion-cultivation and training programs designed to cultivate a more compassionate life. These programs cover the lifespan from birth to death, from "cradle to grave." The book concludes with the benefits of knowing and embracing this more excellent way of life. It asks the question: Do you think this way of life is worthy of your best efforts?

Our survival and the survival of our earth depend on what you and I decide.

## Reflection 1—Reflections on Our Origins/Traditions

I was born on October 7, 1945. Some of my earliest recollections as a toddler and young child in Waycross, Georgia, include: (1) being in my crib at naptime in Mom and Dad's room, just off the living room, scribbling on the wall. I don't recall any harsh or loud words of reprimand. I just remember scribbling on the wall and Mom cleaning it off. (2) At about age five or six, I remember being upset that my dad took my sister, who was one year older than me, to the circus that had come to town, leaving me behind. I remember crying bloody murder and Momma comforting me. I also remember that within a day or two of the circus leaving town, Poochie showed up. Poochie was a female toy terrier and obvious circus dog with a fluffy collar who had been left behind, and I remember walking across the street with "my" dog. (3) I remember playing hide-and-seek with my friends on the block and a group of us hiding in a chest in a garage. The chest had a small hole in the front and was just large enough for one of us (me) to see the seeker. He did find us, and then promptly sat on the top of the chest as we screamed to get out. I guess that is where my bit of claustrophobia originated.

...Experiences of birth, growth, of being, of being loved and secure, becoming, increasing awareness, knowledge, consciousness...of becoming anxious, upset, frightened, even terrified...of death and dying.

In the personal, sketchy, early-developmental stories above, with many years in the interim, I sense some deep truths about the past and future—of the birth of the cosmos, the birth of self, the death of self, and death of the cosmos—apparent physical realities. With the Big Bang, the cosmos was born. Over time over billions of years, life forms evolved, including our hominid species, later, evolving into our own Homo sapiens, a life form aware of itself and able to reflect on its condition, seeking explanations as to what, how, and why life and death. Thus, religion was born.

Upon their return to Jerusalem from Babylonian exile in 535 BCE (before the common era), Hebrew priestly writers and others consolidated the Torah, writing down the oral traditions of the creation story and other stories to help solidify the community of returning peoples. The writers describe in mythological terms an evolutionary truth:

> *"In the beginning when God created the heavens and the earth, the earth was a formless void and darkness covered the face of the deep, while a wind from God swept over the face of the waters. Then God said, "Let there be light;" and there was light. And God saw that the light was good; and God separated the light from the darkness. God called the light Day, and the darkness he called Night. And there was evening and there was morning, the first day."* (Genesis 1:1-5)

Genesis stories like these can be found in all the world's religious traditions. In *Fields of Blood: Religion and the History of Violence,* British author Karen Armstrong describes our earliest human evolution as social animals.[8] She explains humankind's awareness of self, of our tribal beginnings, and of our need for myths (defined as timeless, universal truths) with their hero/heroine characters to explain the unknown, the unpredictable, and potentially dangerous world in which we live. Mythological stories have given individuals and social groups meaning and purpose throughout human history.

In his *"The Hero with a Thousand Faces"*, Joseph Campbell persuasively argues this truth.[9] He describes the journey of the hero/heroine from departure to the "other world," through initiation with its trials and tribulations, and to final reception of the "boon" (e.g., enlightenment, epiphany). The hero/heroine experiences the joy, happiness, and serenity of the boon and resists/refuses to return to the prior world. But then there is a "rescue from without," and the hero/heroine crosses back through the "return threshold" and subsequently masters both worlds, becoming free to truly live.

We hear these myths, and believing them gives us hope, meaning, purpose, and security. We even worship the hero/heroine as a warrior, lover, emperor (even as tyrant), world redeemer, and saint. Hero/heroine images almost always fail as we become aware of our mortality, of our inevitable death with its terrifying reality and truth. But this failure is not always the case, as some myths continue to give individuals and communities meaning, purpose, and freedom, even in the face of death.

One only has to witness our most ancient religious traditions to realize the truth, that religious and philosophic traditions, like myths, give individuals and communities meaning and purpose. They originated in Persia (Zoroastrianism), China (Confucianism, Daoism), the subcontinent of India (Hinduism, Buddhism), the Middle East (Judaism, Christianity, and Islam), and Eastern Europe (Greek philosophical rationalism). The known lives and stories of ancient Axial Age (900 – 200 BCE) giants were significant in human history: Gautama Siddhartha (the Buddha); Confucius; Greek philosophers Socrates, Plato, and Aristotle; and a litany of Abrahamic characters. Their religious and philosophic enculturation of core values such as love, compassion, and the Golden Rule over the last three millennia have contributed significantly to what we consider excellence today.

The Hebrew faith tradition predated Axial-Age experiences and spawned both the Christian and Muslim monotheistic traditions. Influenced significantly by Greek philosophy and Roman dominance in the early Common Era (CE), Christian and Muslim traditions have spread across the known world, becoming the most powerful belief systems of today. Each has produced some of humankind's most excellent and some of its worst experiences, e.g., the Christian Crusades and Islamic terrorism being two of the most dramatic.

Though many today do not accept "religion" in the traditional sense of the word, many recognize and accept our inherent "spiritual" nature and do not deny the positive contributions that the world's religions have made to our common understanding of universal morality and values, which drive our ethical behavior today.

With the rise of the modern era and the scientific method, our knowledge and understanding of life's origins and the evolution of the cosmos have vastly increased. Although our need today for mythological explanation is much less, we still need myth and metaphor to help explain and understand the most complex of scientific information. The work of physicists, chemists, biologists, paleontologists, and archeologists has led to a major increase in our knowledge of how the universe came into being. From a "singularity" (the Big Bang), the earliest atoms, chemicals, and molecules formed all the material of the cosmos, of our world, and of the biosphere we call home, taking over thirteen billion years to be what it is today.

With Charles Darwin's theory of evolution proposed in the mid-1850s, myth collided with scientific fact and historical reality. By no means the only figures in history to do so, biologist Jacque Monod and writer Albert Camus, good friends and co-activists in the French underground during World War II, both contributed significantly to our understanding of our nature, of our physical, mental, and emotional well-being, especially in the context of one of the most traumatic and globally destructive periods in our human history—World War II.

Albert Camus was surrounded by and witnessed the destructive nature of man. He expressed his take on life in his well-known essay, "The Myth of Sisyphus."[10] His experiences led him to question the *purpose* of life, raising the question: Is suicide okay? Monod highlighted his friend's answer at the beginning of his short essay, "Chance and Necessity:"[11]

> "At that subtle moment when man glances backward over his life, Sisyphus returning toward his rock, in that slight pivoting he contemplates that series of unrelated actions which becomes his fate, created by him, combined under his memory's eye and soon sealed by his death. Thus, convinced of the wholly human origin of all that is human, a blind man eager to see who knows that the night has no end, he is still on the go. The rock is still rolling."
> 
> "I leave Sisyphus at the foot of the mountain! One always finds one's burden again. But Sisyphus reaches the higher fidelity that negates the gods and raises rocks. He too concludes that all is well.

*This universe henceforth without a master seems to him neither sterile nor futile. Each atom of that stone, each mineral flake of that night-filled mountain, in itself forms a world. The struggle itself toward the heights is enough to fill a man's heart. One must imagine Sisyphus happy."*

Long before the articulation of the Big Bang theory, Monod presented in his book a compelling argument for how physical reality came about from the earliest atoms and molecules and how life forms developed. He described in some detail how elemental particles, atoms, and molecules came together to form simple chemical substances, and later, more complex chemical substances. He observed that they came together chemically in an extremely specific way, which led Monod to conclude there must be some "cognitive function" at the most elemental level. Moreover, he described some essential truths about the biosphere, about what we see and why we see what we see and experience today. His work inspired me to write the poem, "The Catalyst" below. My wife and I facilitate a compassion integrity training program,[12] and one of the requirements to become a certified facilitator is to develop curriculum engagements for the various skills. Curriculum engagements are developed to lead to critical insight. Engagements include exercises, such as skits, contemplative practices, and reflective writing with mindful dialogues. Whatever the type of engagement, the goal is that the student gains a deeper understanding of the skills. These may be facilitated with the use of a video, a song, a poem, or an appropriate metaphor.

Inspired by Jacque Monod's work in the mid-20th century, and by other materials written since the discovery of the Higgs boson particle and validation of the Higgs field in 2012, I wrote the following poem to be used in a curriculum engagement. I believe it captures the scientific details and essence of what Monod so beautifully and scientifically described in his book. It describes how things came to be— in a quite specific way.

## The Catalyst

*To be, to become...from supersymmetry...Big Bang
Atoms, molecules, a certain way
Not just any way, a certain way.*

*A definite occurrence, yet predictable not,
A definite way, but no one knew why.
The catalyst knew, if listen we would,
To architect, educator, creator itself.*

*Asymmetry it will be, positive entropy delayed,
Discerning best way to create symmetry.
Levo, dextro, which way will it be?
Levo, I think, thus life will it be.*

*Stereospecific and non-covalent, consciousness,
A burning bush not consumed, the way it will be.
Information passed, the arrow of time,
Supersymmetry back to, from whence it came.*

C.O.B

Of course, I give credit to Descartes for paraphrasing his "I think, therefore I am" to "Levo, I think, thus life will it be." Monod's overall thesis of life, of the biosphere, is that it "does not contain a predictable class of objects or events but specifies a particular occurrence—infinite forms most beautiful. He perceived this occurrence as compatible with first principles, i.e., the laws of thermodynamics, although not "deducible" from them, and therefore "essentially unpredictable."[13] Significantly, he goes on to state that life can be partially explained by first principles, but "transcends them in some way, and that other principles applicable only to living systems must be invoked." He believes there is a "cognitive function," what he and others call Maxwell's Demon, explained below.

Integral to his theory of life are three essential properties. The first property is teleonomy, which Monod defines as "all those structures, all the performances, all the activities contributing to the success of the essential project." The second property is invariant reproduction (or simply, invariance); in evolutionary terms, it is species survival. Monod emphasizes that only organic reproduction or invariance can express the third property of his theory, autonomous morphogenesis, implying critical information transfer from one project, one life, to the next. The amount of information transfer depends on the complexity of the biological project or structure being constructed. This latter property along with teleonomy and invariance constitute the three essential properties of all living beings, from single-cell life to complex multicellular life, such as human beings.[14]

Monod continues that though these properties are closely connected, each property is independent. We observe invariance in inorganic crystalline formation—solid salt or sugar crystals and certain crystalline rock formations. Teleonomy and invariance are essential in the formation of any molecular project, whether organic or inorganic. But only life forms express autonomous morphogenesis, the transfer of essential building information from one living generation to the next. Interestingly, Monod believed the property of invariance (reproduction) evolutionarily preceded teleonomy, (i.e., purposeful structuring and functioning required for success). He felt this idea was most consistent with the scientific method of objectivity and impartiality. For Monod, there is no first or final cause, maker, or single intelligent being responsible for life. Many would disagree.

It is noteworthy that when delving into the molecular mechanisms of how organic materials, proteins, and nucleic acids work to make the building blocks of life, Monod is compelled to invoke "Maxwell's demon," (or, I would prefer to say, Maxwell's "angel").[15]

Thus, to drive the molecular point home, so to speak, Monod argues that one cannot explain life phenomena or for that matter any physical structural/functional phenomena that involve stereospecific, non-covalent complexes of symmetrically structured substrates and asymmetrically structured catalysts based solely on first principles, specifically on the second law of thermodynamics. Life formation seems to defy the second law. It is negatively entropic. Monod explains, These phenomena, prodigious in their complexity and their efficiency in carrying out a preset program, clearly invite the hypothesis that they are guided by the exercise of somehow cognitive functions (dare we say a certain level of consciousness?) Using quite complex information.

As I conclude Reflection 1, I hope it has become clear that discovered archeological artifacts, recorded history, religious traditions, myths and metaphors, and earlier scientific discoveries have given us a fairly true picture of how we evolved through time to become the conscious life form we are. We are aware of ourselves and have a rudimentary understanding of the cosmos. We are born, we develop, we have moments of joy and happiness and suffering along the way, and we die. However, it is the scientific method with its objectivity and impartiality that has given us the deepest understanding of how we came to be in this increasingly complex cosmic environment. This then begs the question: What is our true nature as Homo sapiens?

## Reflection 2 — Our True Nature

My wife Conoly and I should not be alive today according to Federal Aviation Administration (FAA) statistics. Our survival, as some might say, must have been "by the grace of God." Well, some said at the time that I must have been a really good pilot to have brought the airplane down the way I did and that both of us survived the crash. Despite my piloting credentials—commercial and instrument rating and flight hours—I think and believe my abilities were not quite the whole truth of why we survived.

*The single-engine Bellanca Super Viking private airplane I partly owned and was flying was fully instrumented and had a great Instrument Landing System (ILS). I loved flying that airplane. Conoly and I were on our way back to Valdosta from a ski trip in late November 1977 near Blowing Rock, North Carolina, where Conoly's parents owned a home. We stopped in Atlanta, Georgia, for me to attend a committee meeting at Georgia Medical Care Foundation. The approach and landing at Charlie Brown Airport, just west of Atlanta, was uneventful. We parked at the private terminal, refueled, and were ready for takeoff home after the meeting that evening. I had patients to take care of the next day in Valdosta. Charlie Brown was an interesting airport, in that its east-west runway had a cliff at the eastern end, requiring the pilot to ascend fairly quickly on takeoff to avoid the cliff's wall.*

*After taking care of the aircraft, we rented a car and left for the three-hour meeting. It was not an especially memorable meeting, but I do remember noticing that the weather outside was changing for the worse, with lowering clouds and some patchy fog beginning to develop. Most pilots are extremely sensitive to changing weather conditions. Daylight was beginning to fade as we returned to the airport.*

# Being And Becoming Excellent - Reflections

After entering the private terminal at Charlie Brown, Conoly waited as I went straight to the weather briefing room to get current and predicted weather in the Atlanta and Valdosta areas. The weather in Atlanta was currently above "minimums" (i.e., 1-mile visibility and 1000-foot cloud ceiling), but with increasing fog, it was predicted to go below minimums within an hour. The weather in Valdosta was to remain Visual Flight Rules (VFR), although the weather between Atlanta and Valdosta would be questionable. I had to file an Instrument Flight Rules (IFR) flight plan. This is a plan that allows you to be under Air Traffic Control's watchful eye for the whole trip. Flying out of Atlanta IFR would be no problem. Flying into Valdosta VFR would be easy. Air Traffic Control (ATC) could vector me around any significant weather between Atlanta and Valdosta. So, "it's a go," as we pilots would say. No sweat. Good plan. Or so I thought.

We are cleared by Ground Control to taxi IFR to runway 090 degrees. We taxi to that runway and await clearance for takeoff by ATC. Soon ATC gives clearance for takeoff. We taxi onto the runway and take off. No problem. We are switched to ATC on another channel and given vectors to take us around Hartsfield International Airport, which is not that far from Charlie Brown (as the crow flies). We are about fifteen minutes into our flight when I detect that the lighted instrument panel is beginning to fade a bit. I know immediately that something is not right. I scan all the instruments and discover that the alternator sensor is registering zero, which means the alternator generating electricity to keep the batteries powered is not working. The FAA determined later that the wire from the alternator to the alternator circuit breaker had come loose. Bottom line: the battery is running down and no "juice" is going in.

I call ATC and declare an emergency. I am losing electrical power, it is already dark outside, and we are above a solid cloud cover with no breaks at all. Not a good situation. ATC clears me back to Charlie Brown, giving steering vectors to get us back as quickly as possible. All airports are below minimums for VFR flights, so I had to make an IFR approach to Charlie Brown. All this requires that electrical power lasts

## Being And Becoming Excellent - Reflections

*long enough to complete the flight back. To save battery power I turn off all panel instruments and lighting that are not required for critical decision-making and begin to make the journey back to Charlie Brown with ATC's help. Conoly is praying silently.*

*We are vectored to a final approach to runway 090 and given clearance for an ILS approach. I'm on the final when all electrical power is lost: no lights, no radios, and no communication with anyone on the ground. The fog is all the way down to the ground. I have no way now of knowing where the end of the runway is. I see some lighting through the fog, but nothing clear enough. I'm thinking, "That cliff is on the other side of the airport. I need to get up above the fog and cloud cover soonest…NOW!" Pilot jargon for doing this is to "wave off." I wave off, still seeing some lights as we ascend back into the clouds. I am now thinking, "Lord, I hope we don't run into Peachtree Tower," a recently built, well-publicized, and very tall building in Atlanta. Fortunately, we rose above the clouds, missing the cliff, missing any tall buildings, but also missing our only chance to land safely on a runway. We find it crystal-clear above the clouds, the moon and stars bright. Hartsfield International Airport is closed. The only way I know this is because there's no airplane traffic into or out of that airport. To the north, I can see some traffic into Dobbins Air Force Base (AFB) near Marietta, Georgia.*

*I'm in a real quandary. I have no contact with anyone on the ground. My instrument panel and all indicators are "dead." I have a flashlight whose light gives us confirmation of what has happened, but that's no real help. I mentally note that my plane has wooden wing spars and four gas tanks within the wings. With no electricity, I know I must manually turn a handle located in the center front flooring to get from one tank of gas to another. And I also remember that this maneuver must be done before the tank runs out of gas or I won't be able to get any gas flow from the other three tanks, each full of gas. There is too much weather between Atlanta and Valdosta for us to head south, though, on the other side of the weather, conditions are visual (VFR), perfect for landing with lights or no lights at the first airport spotted with a lighted runway. I finally decide to stay in the Atlanta area and* fly north, thinking I might be able to maneuver behind one of the airplanes going into Dobbins AFB. Maybe the ground folks will have sent up an airplane to escort us to a known open airport. I hoped.

Maybe I was praying, but honestly, I don't remember. I know Conoly was, silently. She told me later, "I was praying to God that if we were not to make it through this to please take care of Emma and Tommy." Emma, then almost seven years old, and Tommy, five years old, were our two children back in Valdosta. They were staying with their grandmother, whom they called "Gamby," and their Aunt Anne. Conoly was six months pregnant with our third child.

The Bellanca shuddered…I did not get to the gas handle switch on the floor in time…the engine sputtered…then complete silence…no sound whatsoever except the wind over the wings and the propeller turning as the wind flowed through the blades. We are above the clouds, but only for a short distance. Conoly asks, "Are we going down." I answer, "Yes." Complete, total silence…soon, into the clouds, complete darkness. I hear the wind over the wings and get some sense of speed. I must keep the speed above 70 knots or we stall and spin into the ground like a falling rock. If we descend at too sharp an angle, gaining too much speed, our chances of survival when we hit the ground (or whatever) are much reduced. I listen to the wind and adjust the angle of our glide as close to 70 knots as I can determine subjectively. I have nothing else to tell me how fast or how slow we are going, but I know how a stall feels, and we are not stalling—a blessing. "Oh Lord, I can't believe this is all there is to life," is my last thought as we continue to descend.

The last thing I remember was coming out from under the clouds, flying over the tops of a grove of pine trees. We were told later by the FAA investigation team that the plane hit the corner of the roof of a house, then hit a tree, which tore one wing off that had a full tank of gas in it, continued forward to hit another tree, which took off the other wing, and then hit head-on into another tree at about twenty miles per hour, flipping the fuselage of the plane upside-down. That is when I was knocked unconscious, with subsequent retrograde amnesia to all except the grove of pine trees. Conoly remembers it all with only a very brief period of unconsciousness.

*I woke up in the Emergency Department of Kennestone Hospital in Marietta, Georgia. The doctor is sewing up a rather large cut on the left side of my head near the front. I have a broken right ankle, probably due to holding the airplane rudder control until the crash ended the flight. Conoly has a fractured left knee. But that was not the worst of her injuries. The gynecologist could not hear any fetal heart tones, and Conoly felt no movement of the developing fetus. Only later did we know we had lost the pregnancy, and a full month later, Conoly had to be induced to deliver the remains. I use the term "fetus," because at that time neither Conoly nor I were mature enough in our spiritual journey to realize what had happened on a spiritual level. When asked what we wanted to be done with the induced abortion material, which we were told was a girl, it seemed natural then to just have it cremated and disposed of with other "biologic waste."*

*Only later, looking back, did we realize that we had made a deep spiritual mistake. I am sure neither Conoly nor I will ever feel completely reconciled about how we handled our child's physical remains, although we have placed a stone as a memorial of her brief life on our family cemetery plot in Valdosta: many years later, Mary Charles is the name we gave our third child. Our memories go much deeper. But we are both sure of God's unconditional love. With grateful hearts a year and a half later, we had our fourth child, another girl, Lucy Anne.*

*According to the FAA report, we should not be alive today. Given the circumstances, the chance of our survival was less than one in a million. Yes, you could say that I was a very good pilot in the decisions I made that night to keep the airplane straight and level and the airspeed just above stall; or, you could say that the wooden spar wings softened our impact, allowing ease of wing tear that left the gas behind us, thus preventing explosion and fire. Yet, I know that even with those factors, we statistically should not have survived that crash. I am convinced that the Good Pilot, or should I say the Great Pilot, was not me that night; it was the Creator God that night, the one whom I have come to know as the "loving Father," who knew that particular accident wasn't all there was to life, for me or us. What purpose and what end would it have served?*

To state the obvious, mortality is a fact of life. We are not aware of this truth until, like Siddhartha Gautama, the Buddha, we venture forward in life and encounter suffering, aging, and death along the way. Although unconscious at first, the question eventually becomes conscious, and we recognize the deep truth of our nature—we are aware of ourselves: We are born, we grow, we develop, we grow older, we experience joy and suffering, and then we die. The human is unique among living organisms in that it becomes more and more conscious of itself physically, emotionally, intellectually, and spiritually as it moves from birth to youth to adulthood and beyond. Language is key to this developmental process, allowing us to express our unique need to create meaning for our lives.

This truth implies a certain focus on the self – our ego. We have only to remember earlier times in life or observe an infant, toddler, or preschooler to know that primary consciousness is on self—the self's need for food, clothing, shelter, and self need for affirming, nurturing security. Many argue that selflessness is a positive trait only to the degree that selfless acts support the self's needs. Many others argue the contrary, that true selfless acts of sacrifice do exist. Obvious examples include Jesus' sacrifice on the cross, the person who falls on a grenade to save his/her fellow soldiers, or the person who risks death by jumping into the icy water to retrieve a fallen child or beloved animal. The truth of the matter is that responsible relationships with self, with others, and with the environment require us to be both selfish and selfless, depending on the situation and circumstances of the moment. Life and death anxiety, a fact of our self-consciousness, seems to be a driving force: "I can't believe this is all there is to life."

Fear of life and avoidance of its risks, for example, is obvious in the young, curious toddler or child who may stray just so far before returning quickly to the reassuring parent. This gives way dynamically to fear or anxiety of death as our self-consciousness increases. We pass from that childhood period of unconsciousness when we are "invulnerable" and into a level of consciousness where we experience the reality of death to some degree but deny it and seek security from it in a variety of ways. One obvious way is through hero or heroine identification or worship. We admire another person and put that person up on a pedestal. This, we think, is the kind of person we would like to be—a hero or heroine—emulating and believing consciously or unconsciously that this person has the answer to a successful life, a life of purpose and meaning. My biology teacher in high school was just such a heroine for me at that point in my life. Others followed.

In his now classic, 1973 Pulitzer prize-winning *The Denial of Death*, author and social anthropologist Ernest Becker presents a compelling argument for the need for this phenomenon of heroism and its ultimate failure due to the seemingly limitless possibilities on the one hand, yet actual limits of the human experience on the other. Becker states:

> *"When we are young, we are often puzzled by the fact that each person we admire seems to have a different version of what life ought to be, what a good man is, how to live, and so on. If we are especially sensitive, it seems more than puzzling; it is disheartening. What most people usually do is follow one person's ideas and then another's, depending on who looms largest on their horizon at the time. The one with the deepest voice, the strongest appearance, the most authority, and success is usually the one who gets our momentary allegiance; and we try to pattern our ideals after him [or her]. But as life goes on, we get a perspective on this, and all these different versions of truth become a little pathetic. Each person thinks that he has the formula for triumphing over life's limitations and knows with authority what it means to be a man, and he tries to win a following for his particular patent. Today we know that people try so hard to win converts for their point of view because it is more than merely an outlook on life: it is an immortality formula."* [16]

Thus, Becker describes transference, which he asserts is one of man's coping mechanisms to deal with the paradoxical human condition—on the one hand, our partial divinity in creation, yet on the other, the knowledge of our death and decay. The myth of the hero has been historically essential for man to deal with this awareness of self, of this paradox, and to create a viable social and cultural order.

But ultimately, as Becker argues, the hero myth fails, and we have to look beyond self and our paradoxical condition if we are to discover any ultimate meaning of life.

To make this point, Becker contrasts the lives of icons Sigmund Freud and Soren Kierkegaard. He describes in detail the brilliant, but very dogged, self-centered life of psychoanalyst Sigmund Freud. Freud developed a compelling theory of sexuality or instinct theory to explain the human condition and motivation, bringing many bright students such as Carl Jung into his classroom and inner circle. Much to his chagrin, many left that inner circle as further analysis of the human condition showed that his instinct theory did not fully explain human motivation. Though Freud reluctantly admitted in later writings a "death instinct" as part of self's psyche, he was never able to let go of man's creaturely nature, his sexuality, as the primary motivator and meaning in life, which he adamantly held as the standard for psychoanalytic therapy. According to Becker, Freud's character analysis explains much of why he was so dogged about his instinct theory. However, all said, Becker, admits that Freud was "neither better nor worse than other men."[17]

If Freud is Becker's example of psychoanalysis focused on man's physicality as a motivator, then Soren Kierkegaard is his example of psychoanalysis focused on man's spirituality, or consciousness, as a motivator. Kierkegaard, known as the father of existentialism and a well-known 18th-century theologian, preceded Freud, who is considered the father of psychoanalysis. Becker claims Kierkegaard was as much a psychoanalyst as Freud. But unlike Freud, whose foundation of psychology was based upon man's physicality and sexuality, Kierkegaard's foundation was based upon man's character as revealed in the mythical genesis story of the fall of man. Therein, Becker describes a basic truth about our human nature:

> "...this myth [the genesis story] contains...the basic insight of psychology for all time: that man is a union of opposites, of self-consciousness and physical body. A man emerged from the instinctive thoughtless action of the lower animals and came to reflect on his condition. He was given a consciousness of his individuality and his part-divinity in creation, the beauty and uniqueness of his face, and his name. At the same time, he was given a consciousness of the terror of the world and his own death and decay. This paradox is the most constant thing about conscious mankind in all periods of history and society; it is thus the true "essence" of man, as Fromm said. As we saw, the leading modern psychologists...made it the cornerstone of their understanding. But Kierkegaard had already counseled them: 'Further than this psychology cannot go...and moreover it can verify this point again and again in its observation of human life." [18]

Becker hastens to add that this truth of death and decay had one great "penalty" for man: it gave him dread, or anxiety; not just dread or anxiety over the ambiguity itself, but rather dread of "the final terror of self-consciousness, [which] is the knowledge of one's death...a peculiar sentence on man alone in the animal kingdom...that death is man's peculiar and greatest anxiety."[19][20]

Becker further describes the task of the psychoanalyst as one of discovering what defense mechanisms an individual uses to reduce the dread or anxiety which naturally comes from consciousness of self and the knowledge of his/her eventual physical death and decay. One primarily uses the mechanisms of repression and denial. We repress that knowledge into unconsciousness and deny it by seeking security from it in another object. That "object" may be a parent, teacher, mentor, pastor, religious leader, or popular and/or powerful other. Or, the object may be money, power, or fame—in other words, the individual seeks security in someone or something that subconsciously represents immortality or offers the promise of immortality, e.g., the hope presented in the myth of the hero or heroine. The individual transfers this dread or anxiety to this other, temporary though it is. Invariably, the hero falls from the pedestal, and we are again faced with dread and anxiety. The question eventually becomes, "Is there any ultimate meaning to life?" More specifically, "Is there any ultimate meaning to my life?" [21]

According to Becker, Kierkegaard gives an answer that has authority and persuasiveness. His answer necessitates what he calls "the school of anxiety," a schooling that leads to deep psychological and spiritual understanding, where psychology and religion come together. Such a school's curriculum leads to new possibilities, to a new reality, once the self acknowledges and accepts the dreadful knowledge of the futility of adopted repressive and denial defense mechanisms, mechanisms that bind us to finitude. Once acknowledged, we can become open to self-transcendence, and to the ultimate possibility of freedom. Such freedom leads naturally to faith—faith in a "First Cause" of all creation in relationship to an "Ultimate Power," to infinitude. This is in marked contrast to Freud's psychology and psychoanalysis based only on animal instinct, physicality, and sexuality as sole motivators. Becker states,

> *"His [Kierkegaard's] whole argument now becomes crystal clear, as the keystone of faith crowns the structure. We can understand why anxiety "is the possibility of freedom," because anxiety demolishes "all finite aims," and so the "man who is educated by possibility [i.e., the school of anxiety] is educated following his infinity."* [22] *Possibility leads nowhere if it does not lead to faith. It is an intermediate stage between cultural conditioning, the lie of character, and the opening out of infinitude to which one can be related by faith. But without the leap into faith, the new helplessness of shedding one's character armor holds one in sheer terror. It means that one lives unprotected by armor, exposed to his aloneness and helplessness, to constant anxiety."*

In extreme, some view the phenomenon of transference as cowardice, as giving up control, as not facing life and death head-on. Albert Camus might be one of those. As noted earlier in his *The Myth of Sisyphus*, originally published in 1955, Albert Camus posited what he considered psychology's major question: Suicide. [23] Given the human condition, and its absurdity, what is a man to do?

Fall into absolute despair and thus choose suicide? Or accept the absurdity of life with its reality of death and decay, revolt with courage and strength, and free oneself with one's innate physical, intellectual, emotional, and spiritual abilities, as finite and limited as they are, and self-create a life of passionate meaning. Each time the stone rolled down the mountain, the mythical Sisyphus chose to again roll it back to the top of the mountain, again and again, forever. Thus, Camus concluded, "The struggle itself toward the heights is enough to fill a man's heart. One must imagine Sisyphus happy."[24] I am instantly reminded of the poem by William Ernest Henley, "Invictus," written in 1875, which I memorized in the ninth grade of high school and which I can recite to this day:

> *Out of night that covers me,*
> *Black as the pit from pole to pole,*
> *I thank whatever gods may be*
> *For my unconquerable soul.*
> *In the fell clutch of circumstance*
> *I have not winced nor cried aloud,*
> *Under the bludgeonings of chance*
> *My head is bloody but unbowed.*
> *Beyond this place of wrath and tears*
> *Looms but the horror of the shade,*
> *And yet the menace of the years*
> *Finds and shall find me unafraid.*
> *It matters not how strait the gate*
> *How charged with punishments the scroll,*
> *I am the master of my fate*
> *I am the captain of my soul.*

I would argue, as might Becker and Kierkegaard, and even Camus, that Camus' Sisyphus is just another object of transference, as is William Ernest Henley's self. Each is a finite "hero," bound to fall. One might also argue that indeed Kierkegaard's First Cause, Creator, and Ultimate Power is just another object of transference, yet different in being ultimate, unlimited, infinite, and well outside the self and the other, not likely to be toppled. Finally, at bottom, all evidence seems to support the conclusion that repression, denial, and transference, at one level or another, is uniquely human and factually a part of our human nature. It is that part of the life process that deals with the problem of consciousness and human self-awareness of inevitable death and decay. The object or objects of transference one adopts is a matter of necessity with some choice as one grows and develops from birth to death.

This brings me to consider that ubiquitous biologic, bell-shaped curve to which I am naturally led during any discussion of human nature. As with most biological phenomena, our human nature—physical, psychological, emotional, and spiritual—is not simply dualistic, but rather a complex continuum of an individual in context with group sociocultural possibilities, mapping out as a solid, three-dimensional, bell-shaped curve, perhaps skewed in various dimensions, not static, but always dynamic as individuals and groups develop and evolve concerning each other along the arrow of time. One might describe this as the complexification of life processes. We have discovered through scientific methods that even our human observation of the experiments we perform can affect the outcomes. It seems reasonable that this phenomenon might also be true of our observation of our own development and evolution. This is an obvious understatement, pointing to our conscious and subconscious abilities to choose and create. So, any conclusions we make about human nature must consider our observations of it. If we add to this what religious and spiritual leaders have perceived for millennia and what theoretical physicists speculate, we cannot discount the possibility that there is another dimension, a larger reality outside self and the physical world—a transcendent reality and ultimate freedom from our finiteness. This is crudely visualized in Figure 1.

Assuming both science and religion each describe aspects of the BIG truth, there must be connections linking the two ways of thinking and doing. Perhaps the greatest barrier to our correct understanding lies more in language. It seems to me the language of physics does the best job of describing physical reality—particulate and vibrational, quantum and waveform, particles and fields. According to theoretical physicist Sean Carroll, with the discovery of the boson particle in 2012, verifying the Higgs field, we now have a complete description of what physicists call the standard model, mathematical proof that nature is symmetrical. We can now essentially explain in mathematical terms all that we observe in the physical world.[25]

With this most recent understanding, several theoretical physicists, including Sean Carroll, believe there is a "supersymmetry," for which we currently have no solid evidence. It is intriguing to postulate what this supersymmetry might be. For me, perhaps Kierkegaard's concept of "faith" might be the link connecting physical symmetry with supersymmetry suspected by physicists, as suggested in Figure 1. Of course, there is no mathematical formula for "faith." Perhaps "faith" is a mathematical constant like Planck's constant[26] or some such universal factor that expresses a minimal quantum amount of a supersymmetric reality that we humans cannot know or measure from our finite symmetrical reality. I find this interesting to contemplate—two expressions of BIG reality, inseparable, unified, one with symmetry and supersymmetry. Perhaps supersymmetry is the same as the asymmetrical catalyst that brings atoms and molecules together to form symmetrical structures and ultimately form the biosphere we know so well.

Particularly, according to Figure 1, this sphere of "physicality" within which we observe cosmic nature and our own human biological, psychological, emotional, intellectual, and spiritual nature is a symmetrical sphere. It is the finite reality that physicists have described, and which is defined as the Standard Model. This is the reality into which we are born, develop, grow older, and eventually die, all within a postulated infinite supersymmetry along the arrow of time. Within this spherical context there are vast human possibilities, both quantitative and qualitative, that are determined in large part by our genetics but also determined by our own life experiences within a cultural and social order.

From this context come our thoughts; our sense of good, evil, beautiful, ugly, truthful, and false; our speech; and our ethics. Indeed, we can only speculate what lies beyond the symmetrical sphere, though faith traditions give hope for "life" beyond the life we humans have come to know in the sphere.

# Being And Becoming Excellent - Reflections

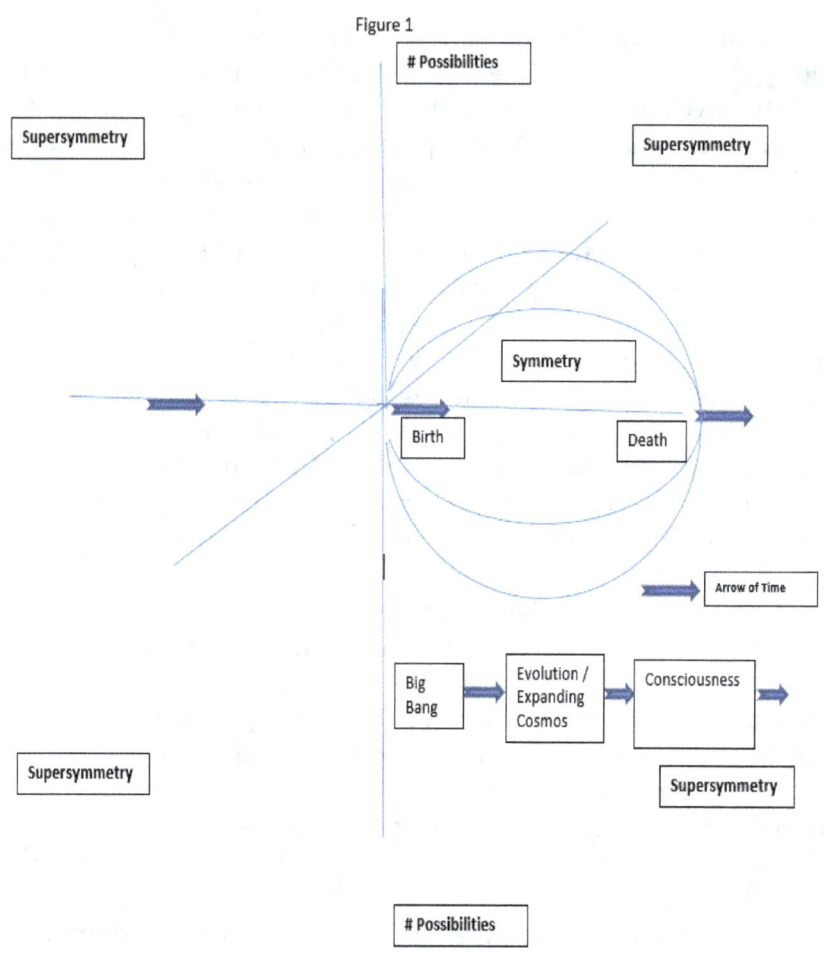

Figure 1

## Reflection 3—On Morality and Ethics

*He who is cruel to animals becomes hard also in his dealings with men.
We can judge the heart of a man by his treatment of animals.*
—*Immanuel Kant*

As regards our current knowledge and understanding of morality and ethics, we must look not only to the great religions of the world and their stories through the millennia, but also to several key figures in the last several centuries. Three come to mind: Immanuel Kant, Jeremy Bentham, and John Stuart Mill. Recently, I added another, Charles E. Curran.[27] Each gives us a glimpse of one or more aspects of a universal being/becoming (ontological) morality and ethic (way of behaving), an ethic that transcends and paves the way to true peace and healing. Just look around. As I write these words, much healing is needed in our world. Inequities, inequalities, injustices, racism, greed, selfishness, power struggles, and wars abound. Given our human nature and all the possibilities of human expression, this is not surprising.

I believe Immanuel Kant (1724 – 1804), a German philosopher, might agree with me on our basic human nature as presented in Reflection 2; it is not simple, but in fact, complex, with many potential combinations and permutations of goodness and badness and everything in between. We, humans, can consciously choose to take the high road or the low road, or unwittingly take some variant in between. At bottom, in Kant's systematic morality and ethics are the reciprocal ideas of human morality and freedom—one implies the other, and both depend on human autonomy. Kant combined our human ability to experience nature through our senses (empiricism) with our ability to reason and to understand cause and effect (rationalism) to argue that it is from our human reasoning and our understanding of natural phenomena that we derive "the general laws of nature that structure all our [physical] experience and give

[us]...the moral law, which is the basis for belief in God, freedom, and immortality."[28] It is only because of our reflective judgment, i.e., the capacity to stand outside ourselves and reflect/observe that we are truly free and autonomous from self to recognize and discern the moral law.

Interestingly, because of our ability to reflectively judge, Kant argued that humanity is "the end point of Nature."[29] I believe Kant is saying Homo sapiens is the only life form whose consciousness has evolved to the point of being able to stand apart from its physical, intellectual, and emotional self, and is thus able to observe and judge itself, i.e., transcend self, becoming autonomous and therefore truly free to discern universal moral truth, the endpoint of nature. For Kant, there is no inconsistency between science, religion, and morality. I agree. Each body of knowledge and experience expresses different aspects of an ultimate Truth – i.e., that consciousness is increasingly becoming aware of itself in the cosmos. (We uncritically speak of the "glory of God," of the Creator. What exactly do we mean by the term "glory," and what is the "glory of the Creator?" Perhaps the Creator's "glory" is becoming fully aware, fully conscious of itself from the Big Bang to the present age. Maybe that is the ultimate meaning and purpose of creation from the beginning – to reach its own "glory.")

For Kant, since we have the will to choose or decide, any action we take involves by necessity a rule or principle of action (maxim). Every action has some goal or objective. The rule or maxim tells us what that goal is and how we will get there. Kant determined that there are two categories of principles (maxims) or rules of action – material and formal. Material rules are those whose object is the satisfaction of a physical desire and how to get to that object. Correspondingly, for Kant, there are hypothetical imperatives, i.e., rules of how one should act in a certain way to get to the object of desire. Keywords are desire and should act. For example, if I desire a donut, I act on the material rule, "if I desire a donut, I go to the donut shop and buy one." The hypothetical imperative is, "if I desire a donut, I should go to the donut shop and buy one."

Kant's formal principles of action (rules/maxims) describe how to act without reference to any desires. As with material rules with their hypothetical imperatives, formal rules have corresponding "categorical imperatives," i.e., commands that one should act in a specific way unconditionally. The difference between a hypothetical imperative and a categorical imperative is that the former applies to me only on the condition that I have willed a desired goal and should act a certain way to obtain that goal; a categorical imperative applies no matter what my goal or desire may be. For Kant, moral laws are categorical imperatives that apply to everyone unconditionally; For example, the moral duty to help others, to not steal, to not kill, to not lie, and to tell the truth apply regardless of whether I have the desire to help others or to steal to increase my bank account or to kill or not kill friend or foe.

In summary, undergirding and overarching Kant's system of ethics are material principles of action, rules or maxims based on desires, goals, and formal principles of action that do not depend on desires or goals and constitute categorical imperatives, i.e., universal commands or laws with which everyone must unconditionally comply. Moreover, according to Kant, when we consciously make material rules or maxims (laws) to achieve desired goals or objectives, we immediately become aware of the moral law. We ask ourselves, "Are there rules, maxims, or laws that are absolute, unconditional? Kant's answer is "yes," and these are the moral laws, laws that depend on the reciprocal ideas of human freedom and morality, which in turn depend on humankind's conscious ability to autonomously reflect on and judge itself. Today, the study of a rules-and-regulations philosophy is known as deontology.

Though there are and have been critics, Kant's system of morality and ethics makes a lot of philosophical and practical sense to me. His system was quite compelling in his time and continues to have a strong influence on our understanding of morality and ethics today.

Likewise, the moral and ethical thoughts of Jeremy Bentham and John Stuart Mill have been and still are today influential in our understanding of morality and ethics. Bentham (1748 – 1832) is best known for his thoughts on morality, the ethics of behavior, and the utilitarian principle, which judges human behaviors based on their consequences. For Bentham, just as the laws of physics explain physicality/nature, the desires for pleasure, happiness, and avoiding pain explain human behavior. This is the basis for a "theory of hedonism," or one might say, "self-centeredness." At bottom for Bentham is the goal of happiness, and happiness is experiencing pleasure and avoiding pain. If a behavior leads to pleasure and/or avoids pain, then one will experience happiness. Viewed from a societal level, one might extrapolate Bentham's theory to a community and hypothesize that the happiness of a community is judged by its overall experience of pleasure and avoidance of pain. Bentham states, " Nature has placed mankind under the governance of two sovereign masters, pain and pleasure. It is for them alone to point out what we *ought* to do, as well as to determine what we *shall* do."[30] Based on these thoughts I am personally led to the conclusion that Bentham's moral philosophy is primarily focused on the self-interest of the individual and of a closely knitted group, such as a family or a local group – what current-day ethical thought might call "in-group." Quite revealing is his description of moral philosophy (ethics) as "the art of directing men's action to the production of the greatest possible quantity of happiness, on the part of those whose interest is in view."[31] John Stuart Mill thought differently and was quite critical of Bentham's moral philosophy.

Mill (1803 – 1873) rejected Bentham's view of human nature as essentially self-centered with narrow self-interest. He believed that human nature included sympathy for others and the desire for perfection.[32] In his *Autobiography,* he claims to have coined the word "utilitarian" in his teenage years, although history attributes the term to Bentham. Mill knew of Jeremy Bentham through his father, who was a friend. For his entire life, Mill believed in the principle of utilitarianism, which he articulated in detail in his 1861 publication *Utilitarianisms.* For Mill, the utilitarian principle is the foundation of all morals. Human behavior is only right in so far as it promotes the happiness of society at large. It is focused on actions rather than on rights or behavioral duties. For example, I may believe a certain behavior is right, but unless it promotes the happiness of society at large, it is not right. Although Mill's system of ethical judgments presumes rules as to what is right and what is wrong, his rules are society's rules rather than self-imposed rules, as described above in Kant's theory of morality. It is probably trite and an oversimplification to summarize Mill's moral and ethical philosophy of utilitarianism as "right action is that action which produces the greatest happiness for the greatest number of people." Yet, that statement is invariably attached to the work of John Stuart Mill. His moral philosophy is goals-oriented, the study of which is known today as *teleology*.

On reflection, the ethical philosophies of Kant, Bentham, and Mill, as they have been understood and applied over the last three centuries, have left many thinkers of moral philosophy in a quandary. Our world has become much smaller and more complicated since Kant and Mill. With our dramatic and tragic experience of evil and good over the last couple of centuries, along with our worldwide instant communications, life for individuals and groups has become easier and yet more complex, making an absolute rule (deontological) or a goal (teleological) ethic wanting in our ethical relationships today.

What might be an optimal ethics model today? Riane Eisler, a social theorist, and activist gives us a glimpse in her book, *Nurturing Our Humanity*. She expertly builds the case for partnership relationships rather than domination relationships, which have been and still are the norm in our global society. She argues that the key to transforming from a dominance ethic to a partnership ethic lies in individual and community awareness of our common humanity and interdependence.[33] Implied in her work is the need for a practical, relationships-based ethic. What might this look like? How would it work? Charles E. Curran, in *"The Catholic Moral Tradition Today: A Synthesis"*, gives us an idea.

Curran presents a brief, clear, and concise summary comparing the three best-known historical ethical models - Kant's deontological model, and the two teleological models of Bentham and Mill. He identifies positive contributions as well as shortcomings of each when applied to today's human situation.[34] As noted above, these models became the standard moral and ethical systems in the 20th-century legal, economic, political, social, and cultural life of individuals and communities. Curran goes on to compare a more recent third model, H. Richard Niebuhr's responsibility model.

# Being And Becoming Excellent - Reflections

Niebuhr describes his model in The Responsible Self, published in 1963.[35] According to Niebuhr, each of us is morally and ethically responsible for our thoughts, feelings, and actions toward self as well as toward others and the environment. This responsibility ought and must be considered in our relationships. Curran further develops Niebuhr's model by combining his necessary responsibility component with a relationality component into a system of ethical behavior that he believes better accounts for the 21st-century's more complex, interconnected, interdependent world. The relationality/responsibility model will be taken up in more detail in Reflection 4.

For completion's sake and before proceeding with Curran's comparative analysis of the three ethical models above, I would like to parenthetically mention an ethical theory developed by Joseph Fletcher, an Episcopal priest turned atheist, in his 1966 book, Situation Ethics – The New Morality.[36] In thoughtful circles, situation ethics in theory and practice was gaining popularity before his publication but it became even more popular as an ethical model in the years following. It peaked in the 1970s and declined thereafter, viewed by most ethicists then as an "anything goes" ethical theory, an ethic likely oversimplified and mislabeled as one based on absolute individual self-autonomy with no absolute moral rules or regulations.

The BBC's Ethics Guide summarizes the good and bad points of Fletcher's ethics:

> "In situation ethics, right and wrong depend upon the situation. There are no universal moral rules or rights; each case is unique and deserves a unique solution. Situation ethics rejects 'prefabricated decisions and prescriptive rules.' It teaches that ethical decisions should follow flexible guidelines rather than absolute rules and [should] be taken on a case-by-case basis".[37]

The Guide goes on to state that situation ethics is both "good" and "bad." It is personal, particular, and based on doing good, all "good" elements. The "bad" elements include an absence of most universal moral truths, lack of clarity on such definitions as "love", and difficulty to implement. The article further cites a statement by ethicist Daniel Callahan in The Hastings Center Report of 2000, "Universalism and Particularism." He stated that "by the 1970s situation ethics had been roundly rejected as no ethics at all…." However, many ethicists today might disagree with Callahan's overall assessment.[38]

Returning to Curran's comparative analysis, let's begin by first taking up Kant's deontological model. In summary, this model is all about duty, law, and obligation, and is best exemplified by Kant's categorical imperative and the universality principle as described previously. A person can do anything so long as they accept the maxim that anyone else in similar circumstances may do the same. A simple present-day example might be the question of the use of alcohol in underage military recruits who may be placed in harm's way but are not allowed to drink alcohol. Right or wrong? According to the maxim, the answer might be that it is "right" for the underage recruit to drink alcohol in moderation, reasoning that "the underage recruit is potentially required to give up his or her life for the country. Why can they not drink alcohol in moderation?" Mill's utilitarian (teleological) principle would justify the use of moderate alcohol in the underage as "right" based on the pleasure and happiness principle, i.e., actions are right in proportion as they tend to promote happiness (pleasure), wrong as they tend to produce the reverse of happiness (pain).

Others would say it is "wrong" because we know empirically that underage recruits are more likely to have problems with alcohol than those of drinking age. Furthermore, the military lends more toward Kant's ethic to follow the rules and regulations, do one's duty, be responsible and meet one's obligations, and follow the orders of his/her superiors and the Commander in Chief. This stance is all in the name of "military good order and discipline." This means following the law: no alcohol until legal age is obtained. The same ethical analysis could be applied to the use of marijuana, although currently, the drug is illegal at any age in the military by federal law. Thus, herein lies the natural tension between the two models.

Curran continues by describing the shortcomings of Kant's rules and regulations ethic. He uses examples from Christian scripture of love, mercy, and compassion that reflect day-to-day Catholic practice. But this in many ways contradicts Catholic Church dogma/doctrine as established, interpreted, and enforced by its Magisterium authority. However, Curran does admit that the authoritarian model has some strengths. He summarizes:

> "It upholds objectivity, disagrees with subjectivism and relativism, and prevents the individual from making personal exceptions, thus combating the danger of individualism so prevalent in our society. However, the problems intrinsic to the authoritarian model argue against making it the primary model for moral theology and Christian ethics".[39]

Curran believes what is needed is a universal moral system of ethics.[40]

He then turns to an analysis of Mill's teleological model of behavior, i.e., we strive for the greatest good, the goal. Whereas deontology emphasizes laws, duties, and obligations and speaks of doing what is "right," teleology is all about goals or ends and speaks of doing what in the end is considered "good." Curran rightly argues that in our day-to-day activity, we usually operate in a goal-oriented way. We set a goal or goals and then decide "how," or how we will obtain the goal or "good." Interestingly, Curran goes on to cite and discuss in some detail the complex and very detailed ethical system of 13th-century theologian Thomas Aquinas (1225 – 1275 CE) as the best example of a teleological approach embraced by the Roman Catholic tradition.[41] He cites other examples, which include the Social Gospel school of Walter Rauschenbusch and the situation ethics of Joseph Fletcher. Each ethic is goal-oriented, with goodness or rightness depending only on the final consequence of the action(s) taken. If the end result is good for the self (achieves pleasure and avoids pain), then the action toward it is good. This is known as consequentialism. Extended to a greater number (society), Curran explains that utilitarianism is a subset of consequentialism. For the utilitarian, if the action leads to the greatest good for the greatest number of people, then the action is good.

According to Curran, utilitarianism has three serious drawbacks. First, the model runs the risk of putting the individual in an unacceptably lower priority concerning "the greatest good for the greatest number." Curran cites the case of economic issues. For example, having a high gross national product does not necessarily ensure equitable distribution to "the greatest number of people." So, how we get to the goal (action or actions) becomes as important as the goal itself. The risk is failing to consider individual human rights.

Second, Curran argues, "utilitarianism shares with all consequentialisms the basing of morality only on consequences." Universal moral values, such as truth-telling, not lying, not killing, and keeping promises can be put aside as long as the outcome, the desired end goal is achieved. Utilitarians recognize that keeping promises makes for good outcomes, but there is no emphasis placed on loyalty or attachment to the other to whom the promise is made. So, if the end goal is such that breaking the promise will more likely lead to the desired greatest good, then breaking the promise is justified, as long as "no one has to know that the promise has been broken."[42]

Finally, the third set of objections to utilitarianism centers around the motivation or intentionality of the means to a desired end (goal). Thus, it is insufficient to simply view the desired end, but rather necessary to consider by what means and by what causes the goal was accomplished. For example, Curran cites the moral evaluation of the act of killing. Was the act "intentional, accidental, or by not acting when it was morally impossible to act?"[43]

Curran concludes that advocates of consequentialism and utilitarianism are aware of these objections. As a result, some have modified the model to incorporate rules—aka "rule utilitarianism"—which is likely to result in more optimal consequences. This is in contrast to "act utilitarianism," which "occasionally justifies actions that most people would intuitively oppose."[44]

In summary, based on the work of Curran and others in the late 20th century, along with the earlier work of Immanuel Kant, Jeremy Bentham, and John Stuart Mill, humanity has made significant, positive steps in consciousness toward what constitutes an optimally moral and ethical life. However, many today believe that these models fall short of our need for a more universal practical ethical system, one that considers not only the well-recognized universal moral principles and norms applied individually and communally, but also considers the dynamic nature of our being and becoming as individuals in an increasingly complex local and global community.

What appears to be needed is an ontological (having to do with being and becoming), ethical model of morality, a transforming ethic that addresses the dynamics of human development in responsible relationships with self and with others. By "others," I refer to other human beings, other living beings, as well as other organic and inorganic matter (our environment, our home planet), and the cosmos. We need a theory and practice of behavior that considers the dynamic complexity of our uniqueness and our responsible relationship with others in the context of a diverse, interconnected, and interdependent global community.

## Reflection 4—Relationality/Responsibility Ethics

A Transforming Ontological Ethic

*Recalling a time of strained relationship, loneliness...a time of pain...a time of darkness...of personal and community responsibility... I can't completely explain it. I'm not even sure I am recalling the event with complete accuracy, but what I distinctly remember was that I felt alone, actually felt abandoned, with no one alongside to face that dark time. The vision I remember is like a dream. I am in a dark hallway of the hospital, just outside the medical records room, the hallway that led to both the psychiatric ward and the doorway for the Doctors' parking lot outside. I was chief of staff of the hospital, having been elected by the medical staff. One of my community responsibilities was to monitor the professional behavior of credentialed physician staff.*

*One physician, Dr. X, was a highly competent, capable, and dedicated internal medicine physician. One might even say he was too dedicated. His patients worshiped him. He was like a little "god" to them. He made it a point of pride to do rounds earlier than any other staff physician and would defend his patients in a way that many times resulted in the severe denigration of other physicians and nurses, which he would document in the medical chart. When he made a recommendation, he expected his patients to comply without fail. One of his requirements was that each of his patients always carries on their person a summary of their medical problems and a list of medications. If they presented to the ER with a problem that was not a true emergency and without the required information on their person, he would send them back home to retrieve the information. In a real emergency, of course, he would see and take care of them emergently, but after the care was given and the patient was stable, he often gave the unfortunate patient a thirty-day notice to find another doctor. At times, his behavior was not only disruptive but extreme and judgmental. He'd point fingers at colleagues and write inappropriate notes in the medical record concerning staff.*

*He had been doing this for years and somehow each time managed to reconcile one way or another, with a flower or gift or an apologetic word after the acuteness of the incident. But this time, the incident was quite serious. The nursing staff had brought it to the nursing director's attention, and she had brought it to me as chief of staff. Several issues were involved, one professional and one personal. First and foremost was a patient safety issue, an issue urgent enough and serious enough that I could not permit Dr. X the benefit of the doubt. The other was the complicating issue that Dr. X and I covered each other's practices when the other was "off call" or out of town. We had been in this arrangement for several years. I cared very deeply for Dr. X and considered him a personal friend, despite his shortcomings. However, as chief of staff, I had no choice but to immediately and summarily suspend his hospital privileges until an investigation could be conducted. Essentially, I was bringing into question our relationship, personal and professional. This was acutely painful and had a deep and personal effect on me. I felt profoundly alone. I can't explain why I felt this severe loneliness, a feeling I can only describe in the extreme as abandoned by God, in darkness, with no one with me completely estranged. The only other time I felt the same level of darkness and estrangement was in the literal "darkness" Conoly and I experienced during our private airplane crash in November 1977.*

There have been many similar situations in my life as son, brother, husband, father, grandfather, and leader of several different organizations, situations when the complexity of relationships posed difficult questions like, "How should I respond? What is the right thing to do? What is the best response in this situation?" A rules-and-regulations approach (deontological), although helpful at times, was insufficient. Neither sufficient was a lofty end-goals approach (teleological), although it can be helpful at times. And neither sufficient was making or allowing a unilateral, autonomous, independent, anything goes decisions approach (situational), although tempting. For me, none of these ethical approaches have proven adequate by themselves to resolve thorny ethical dilemmas. However, I have found that an approach that considers both individual and group responsibilities and relationships at the same time leads to the most optimal decision(s) regarding actions and behaviors. From a philosophical, ethicist perspective, this approach is what I would best describe as *ontological* (a being and becoming ethic).

The term "ontological" is key. It categorizes the very essence of what this book is about: the reflection or the account of human nature as being and becoming excellent in responsible relationships with self and with others. Human beings are sentient life forms, physically, emotionally, and spiritually able to reflect upon ourselves as to who we are and what we will become or not. Beyond this statement, the study and use of the term can get complicated. It has a history dating back to the 1600s, with its first known use by English philosopher Gideon Harvey, which was popularized as a philosophical term by German philosopher Christian Wolff.[45] The root terms of the word come from the Greek word *on* or *eimi,* meaning "being" and from *logos,* meaning "study" or "account." Thus, *ontology* literally means "the study (or account) of being."

As already described in Reflection 3, the comparative analysis of the three historical ethical models by theologian-ethicist Charles Curran is both instructive and informative, leading to what he named the "relationality-responsibility model" of ethics.[46] I believe this model answers today's need for a more universal, transformative, and practical moral ethic. When integrated with the values of love and compassion, forgiveness, reconciliation, and restoration, the ethic can lead to true peace and healing.[47] One only has to look at Northern Ireland and South Africa experiences to see this.

Curran admits this relationality-responsibility model is universal, but then he specifically applies the model only within the Catholic tradition.[48] Decontextualized from Catholicism, the model he describes is, I believe, truly universal and therefore can be applied to the entire human condition, religious and non-religious. In fact, H. Richard Niebuhr emphasizes the universal, philosophic character of the responsible self, although he, too, discusses this only in a Christian context.[49] Curran takes many of Niebuhr's ideas of responsibility, adds and develops the relationality component, which he then particularizes to the Catholic tradition.

Niebuhr begins his essay by introducing the word "responsibility." It is a word that has taken on different meanings throughout history, from Aristotelian ethics to current-day ethical systems. Niebuhr then discusses the root meaning of the word as a complex symbol, a symbol of man, "the maker," (responsible toward some good or goal "telos," according to the principles of teleology), of man "the civilian" (responsible toward doing what's right according to principles of deontology), and of man "the one who does what's fitting," who is responsible toward the unique situation. Niebuhr then recognizes the need for clarity as he writes:

> "The idea of responsibility, if it is to be made useful for the understanding of our self-action needs to be brought into mind more clearly than has been done by these preliminary references to its uses in past theory and common experience. Our definition should not only be as clear as we can make it; it should, if possible, be framed without the use of symbols referring to the other great ideas with which men have tried to understand their acts and agency. Only so will it be possible for us to develop a relatively precise instrument [model] for self-understanding and also come to an understanding of the instrument's possibilities and limitations."[50]

Curran summarizes Niebuhr's clarification of this "instrument," or model.

According to Curran, the responsibility model or instrument consists of several components. These include response to an action upon us based on our interpretation of the question, "What is going on?" with a willingness to be accountable for any response to our response, all in solidarity with the continuing community of agents. Curran then quickly expands the model by "calling persons to initiate action as well as [to] respond to the actions of others."[51] This model or instrument of responsibility applies to both individuals (me and you) and to groups (informal support groups/study groups and formal organizations, city governments, nations, et al)

More on point for us—and from a philosophical perspective—Curran's understanding of this model with its relationality component can be best summarized in his own words:

> "…. Consider the great diversity and particularity existing in our world. In the midst of such diversity the deontological and teleological models do not seem adequate. There appears to be no detail law that all people should follow. There seem to be no built-in ends or goals that all should seek. However, in this situation, the danger arises that everyone does one's own thing. Some type of relationality-responsibility approach seems to be the best way to avoid tribalism and chaos in the midst of the particularity and diversity of our global existence today.[52] … Earlier this volume recognized both the Catholic emphasis on universality and the importance of a historically conscious approach. The relationality-responsibility model interpreted in the light of catholicity i.e., (universality) fits the historical consciousness approach with its greater emphasis on historicity, change, individuality, and contingency and its unwillingness to let go of some general universal morality common to all humankind. Neither the deontological nor the teleological model can account as well for the diversity, historicity, and contingency which characterize so much of our life today."[53]

To conclude this Reflection and to introduce Reflection 5, I will here attempt to describe and apply the relationality-responsibility model in a more universal context, using a thought experiment.

The experiment theorizes that a newborn human comes into the world with certain genetic information that immediately begins expressing itself in early developmental physical, emotional, mental, and spiritual traits in relation to self, to others, and to community/society and environment. These expressions have an attendant rudimentary level of responsibility, if not conscious (e.g., an infant crying in response to not being attended to in a timely manner for a diaper change, for much wanted/needed food, or warmth from the cold, i.e., clothing and shelter, or for the much-needed security touch of the other).

Growth and development occur within real-time situations, i.e., "contingencies" that are good or not so good given our human nature as described in Reflection 2, and within the context of parental, cultural, socioeconomic, and political conditions. In this way, the structure and content of the individual human being begin to form and are continuously forming, being, and becoming, as the level of general consciousness increases, and individual life experiences become ever more complex.

Herein lies the problem: No matter where the individual is along the arrow of time in life's journey, the individual brings a unique, real-time personal structure and content into a relationship that filters the relational experience, prejudging (consciously or unconsciously) positive or negative, safe or unsafe, and requiring certain responses on a continuum—positive, negative, or neutral. This is further complicated by the fact that the individual is most likely not fully conscious of her or his structure and content, or at best has an inadequate understanding. Because of this and due to the reality of individual diverse structures and contents and the need for security within very different cultures, societies, and religions, it follows that such relationships will only be truly mutual, responsible, caring, and compassionate if the individual is willing to "dethrone" his / her constructed self with its content and "put another there."[54]

Thus, the responsible self must first become conscious of this truth about its formative nature and limitations and then be willing to deconstruct itself, at least to some degree, thereby opening itself to a more mutual relationship with the other. This requires a certain degree of mentally emptying oneself (the Greek term *kenosis* applies), opening oneself to the other, and putting oneself "in the shoes of the other" (empathizing). In essence, empathizing is taking on the structure and content of the other. Of course, for such relationships to actually occur and mature responsibly, all selves involved must do the same. Simply stated, "All involved must be willing to be open to themselves and each other."

The Christian tradition has a divine example, as written by Paul of Tarsus in his letter to the Philippians 2:5-8:

*5 Let the same mind be in you that was in Christ Jesus,*
*6 who, though he was in the form of God,*
   *did not regard equality with God*
   *as something to be exploited,*
*7 but emptied himself,*
   *taking the form of a slave,*
   *being born in human likeness.*
   *And being found in human form,*
*8 he humbled himself*
   *and became obedient to the point of death—*
   *even death on a cross.*

How exactly does this process take place, consciously or unconsciously?

Reflection 5 and a set of stories by medical students from the biomedical arena, taken from Vital Report Reflections (VRR), may contribute to a deeper understanding.

## Reflection 5—Application of the "New" Ethics

There really is not anything new about the relationality-responsibility ethic. We have unconsciously known about it all along and have been practicing it at some level. Because of the explosion of information in the last half century and because of instant communication around the world, only recently have we become more conscious of the need to intentionally apply this ethic in our increasingly complex lives in relation to the increasingly complex "other." This awareness of complexity compels us to reexamine our individual and community relationships and responsibilities and to be intentional about how we act in such an interconnected, interdependent global community.

Nowhere is this need for a relationality-responsibility ethic more than in the medical/healthcare domain. The following three medical student clinical reports, serendipitously presented to me on the same day, are examples of this need.[55] These also reflect our basic human nature, a nature previously discussed, one that can create real barriers to optimal, compassionate relationality-responsibility toward self and others. Such action requires intentionality and great courage to overcome these barriers.[56]

### *CT reflects on a Family Medicine rotation experience:.*

> Our paents interact with many dierent people while receiving care, from med students to physicians, nurses to case managers, and social workers to therapists. Especially during a hospitalizaon, I oen feel bad because paents must tell the same story again and again, and I marvel at how they can keep track of all the dierent people who come to talk to them. But one thing that struck me during my family medicine rotaon was that, while I may

*have assumed the patient was telling the same true story to everyone, this is not always the case.*

*On inpatient week (in-hospital setting versus outpatient setting), I saw a man who was post-op day one after getting a colostomy (a procedure for diverting fecal material through the abdominal wall, away from the rectal area) for really bad sacral ulcers that had begun to form fistulas [fecal tracks from the rectum through the ulcer areas] with the rectum. The idea was that the colostomy would give the ulcers time to heal. So, I visited him in the morning. He was a pleasant man with a Southern accent, who was experiencing heartburn and was worried about his distended abdomen. He was sweet to me and patient with my questions and clarifications, given my limited access to the electronic medical record (EMR). We talked about his heartburn and how the blow-up bed he was on made it difficult to sit up, but that he was feeling much better after getting sips of water. And he was eager for the surgeons to come to check on his distended abdomen. I finished up with a few more questions about how he was doing, and it was overall a quite positive interaction, in my opinion.*

*Later, after presenting his case in table rounds, we were on the third floor doing bedside rounds. Our attending was busy, and a case manager came up, wanting to talk about my patient. I said I was familiar with him and could relay any information to the attending. The case manager proceeded to paint quite a different picture of my patient than I would have expected. She asked if we were going to put him on long-term antibiotics, because if he needed to be at a skilled nursing facility, then that was going to be a problem. Evidently, he had a poor relationship with many care facilities and had a history of checking out of one specific facility with his girlfriend only to come back twelve hours later with dirt in his ulcers and a positive drug screen. The case manager then implied something quite unprofessional about how he got dirt/gnats in his sacral wound and called him an arrogant SOB. [I will not clarify this...you get the point] – C.O.B. I'm standing there a bit stunned at this point, thinking that we should not be talking about patients in this manner. She finished by saying that she just wanted to warn me about him and walked away. Nobody else seemed to have heard what she said, not even my attending, so I updated him with her concerns in as purely factual a way as I could. But the incident left me reflecting: How was it possible that the two of us got such different impressions about the same patient? Perhaps my impression was a bit naïve and uninformed—it was my first day seeing him. I didn't know much at all about his history, nor had I heard anything about his relationship with care facilities. I hadn't asked him to do anything difficult or anything he didn't want to do.*

*Yet, I must think that the case manager had it a bit wrong, too; unless the patient was quite manipulative, he couldn't be all bad, as she was making him out to be. There are innumerable reasons why this case manager could have been upset with him, but none of them seemed a good enough reason to speak about him as she did.*

*In the end, I learned that kindness goes a long way. Even with frustrated patients, if you treat them with respect and listen to their concerns without allowing a tone of impatience or defensiveness to enter your voice, you can turn an encounter around. Health problems can be scary and frustrating. It did not seem that this case manager was being kind to this patient, at all. It seemed that she had heard enough or had enough interactions with him to deem him unworthy of her kindness and respect. I hope never to reach a point like that with any of my patients in the future.*

CT exemplifies empathy; she put herself in the other's position and identified as much as a person can with another's feelings, thoughts, actions, and situations. This is possible to one degree or another, but obviously, it is impossible to identify with the other 100 percent. In this case, CT identifies in general with the patient who must undergo multiple encounters with medical students, interns, and residents, as well as with their attending (primary provider), all of whom have their turn at medical evaluation and reporting. This is all part of the training program for students and apprentices in the healthcare field. CT feels for the patient who "has to tell his story over and over again." Thus, a relationship is formed, and responsibilities are defined early in the patient's journey through hospitalization, which is unique in each healthcare setting. In this case, it appears a "good" relationship is established between CT and the patient.

Along comes the social worker, who already has an established relationship with the patient, one that appears from CT's perspective to be quite different from her own. The whole ethic of truth-telling is raised, along with specific questions: Is the patient telling CT the full truth about what has led to this hospitalization? Has he failed to comply with the doctor's orders? Has he, in fact, used drugs and allowed the ulcers to worsen? CT's reflections do not give us the answers, but the social worker's experience and input about the patient would lead us to believe he has not been fully truthful. Moreover, the social worker's attitude about her relationship with the patient in the outpatient environment raises additional questions about her compassion for herself or himself, compassion for others, and the potential issue of "empathic distress," a common and well-known issue for healthcare workers.[57]

More important, how can one, in this case, CT, recognize and understand the potential for empathic distress in the other (the social worker), and become empathetic, "putting oneself in the social worker's shoes," resonating emotionally and relating in a way that is responsible and leads to optimal compassionate care of the patient and the healthcare team (doctors, nurses, social workers, students)? In this case, "optimal" may mean "tough love" compassionate truth-telling encounters with the patient and healthcare workers, both during the hospital stay and as discharge planning to longer-term care takes place. Such is the mix of human nature, the reality of our human condition, and the need for a relationality/responsibility ethic based on love and compassion, forgiveness, reconciliation, and restoration.

### *SP's reflection*

SP beautifully demonstrates the pathways to an optimal relationality-responsibility ethic.

> *The first week of my transplant surgery service, I got a text around eight PM that we were flying out on an organ harvest at*

midnight. I was excited—it was my first surgery on this service, my first private jet plane ride, and my first ride in an ambulance. We were the liver/kidney team, and we arrived at the site before the heart team. Anesthesia had not yet arrived, and the patient was not yet in the OR. While we waited, my attending chatted with me about how organ harvests can be very emotional experiences, especially this one. In fact, if I wasn't emotionally moved today, he said I was probably in the wrong profession. He recommended that I should feel free to step out and take a break if needed. I assured him that I would be fine. The heart team arrived, and we all went back to the OR. The OR room felt small and cramped, and there were at least twenty people in there—moving things, strapping things, typing on computers, dropping things on sterile tables. It was hard to hear exactly what was going on. A small crowd was gathered around the patient, helping prepare for the harvest.

When this crowd moved away, I immediately noticed a small child, lying naked and intubated on the OR table. I talked with a nurse and was told that the four-year-old girl was brain dead from a car crash five days before, and the family had recently decided to donate all her intra-thoracic/abdominal organs. Suddenly, I felt queasy—or uncomfortable? It was some overwhelming fraction of grief the parents will always feel. When everyone was scrubbed in, the room became silent. A woman in the room spoke. "Let us all take a moment of silence to honor the life of [patient name]." For about thirty seconds, the room was deafeningly silent, completely still. After the surgery began, I nodded to my attending and stepped out into the hallway to take a break. On the way home, my attending was incredibly kind to check in on me and talk with me about dealing with patient death. I became very aware that many surgeons must face patient death regularly, and perhaps without the emotional support I was given. How can we prevent/lower emotional distress and burnout in these physicians?

A 2018 article by Kapoor et al studied the impact of a "sacred pause" to honor the life of a deceased patient. Out of 34 ICU team members surveyed, 79 percent of the respondents felt that this pause helped bring closure and overcome feelings of distress and grief. However, only 55 percent felt that this pause would help prevent burnout. The National Hospice and Palliative Care Organization (NHPCO) surveyed 390 hospice staff workers and found that personal rituals after the deaths of their patients helped them cope with their grief (71 percent) and prevented burnout. Personal rituals included a broad range of activities that honor the death of a patient—creating small gifts for the family of a deceased patient, holding yearly memorials, putting up wreaths for each patient lost, etc.

A 2015 study by Schulman et al introduced "Patient Death Debriefing Sessions" into an inpatient oncology rotation at Memorial Kettering Cancer Center to address the emotional reactions that residents have after the death of their patients. The ten-minute sessions were completed within forty-eight hours of a patient's death and were led by an attending physician. Seventy-nine residents were surveyed, and a majority found that the sessions helped support them emotionally after a patient's death. I would suggest the implementation of patient death debriefing sessions in all teaching centers.

Acknowledging our grief and talking about it can help us find closure without becoming burnt out or numb to the experiences faced in medicine each day. Rituals to honor the death of patients can help keep the memory of a lost patient alive and provide acceptance of a patient's death. Despite the turmoil of emotions, I felt at the time, I look back on this experience with gratitude. I was able to witness an incredibly selfless gift. Both the moment of silence in the OR before the procedure and the debriefing with my attending afterward brought me closure and helped me feel emotionally supported during this time, such that I am fully able to feel the loss of this patient, accept her death, and move forward.

In the *Oxford Handbook of Compassion Science*, Stephen Porges proposes a "multistep, sequential model" that optimizes the effects of "contemplative training, leading to a greater capacity to feel and express compassion." Such a model includes 1) a safe context, 2) performance of rituals such as prayer, meditation, chants, dance, 3) contemplative training, and finally 4) experiencing compassion and a sense of oneness.

This case is a good example of Porges' multistep sequential model. First, the harvesting surgeon has created a "safe" environment in which SP can experience this tragic set of circumstances and can better deal with the reality of our human condition—we all die. The surgeon-mentor gently prepares SP by giving her permission at any point during the procedures "to step out" of the operating room, to take a break if needed, which SP did at one point. Second, the operating room staff performed a calming ritual. The experienced nurse had everyone in the room pause for thirty seconds of silence to honor the life of this child, acknowledging the supreme gifts being given by the child and her parents.

Third, after the operating room experience and after their return to the receiving facility, the surgeon took time to check on SP to make sure she was okay. He "stress debriefed" the incident with SP. This allowed SP to tell her story, to contemplate and reflect in writing the experience and overall meaning in the medical school training context. Finally, SP felt she had experienced an "incredible selfless gift" to herself—both in the moment of silence in the operating room and in the surgeon's genuine concern demonstrated by debriefing and checking on her to make sure she was okay. SP experienced true compassion, and maybe even a sense of "oneness" with the child, the team, and the surgeon. She was grateful. Having had this optimally positive experience, SP came away thinking that "patient death debriefing sessions should be implemented in all teaching centers." She had experienced true compassionate action and saw the benefit of implementing such a program at all levels of healthcare education and training. The surgeon had appropriately and compassionately established a *responsible relationship* with the medical student, the very essence of a relationality-responsibility ethic.

### *JW's reflection*

The following reflection by JW illustrates the need for medical ethics education and training of all healthcare workers as part of the standardized curriculum, and it illustrates the compelling need for the

## Being And Becoming Excellent - Reflections

cultivation of the kind of relationality-responsibility ethic exemplified in the previous reflection.

> The patient, JG, was thirty-seven and the father of two teenagers, fourteen and sixteen years old. He was married to his wife of nineteen years. He had worked as a mechanic from the age of sixteen until he was laid off two years ago. He wasn't aware of any medical problems he may have had. He had been drinking eight beers every day since he was seventeen, however, nobody had told him it was wrong. Not until he ended up in the hospital..
>
> JG was my first patient on the Neurology consult service at University Hospital. Well, he wasn't even my patient, really; we were just a consulting service. I didn't even feel particularly drawn to him personally as I talked to him about his history and performed an exam as I had on the last dozens, if not hundreds, of patients I've seen in my last year. Sure, I thought his story was sad, but I had just finished two weeks of CMC neurology, where multiple times a day we dealt with babies who wouldn't live past a year. In a sense, I was already jaded as a medical student. The only thing I remember being particularly interested in was how floridly jaundiced JG was and how I was looking forward to finally getting some liver and GI pathology after spending four months away from medicine..
>
> After that initial consult visit, I never got to talk to JG again. He went for an esophagogastroduodenoscopy (EGD), a procedure to study the upper gastrointestinal tract later that day, and as a precaution for aspiration from potential GI bleed, he was to remain intubated just for the night. However, when I stopped by his room, he remained intubated. Because of his EGD, he never got to get the EEG and MRI that we recommended. I remember feeling a little thankful for this as now I could pick up another patient to work-up. The next day, he remained intubated and had ST elevations on EKG. The next day, during table rounds, we decided we were going to sign-off until the MRI and EEG were performed because otherwise, we had nothing to add. Because of this, we had to see him on bedside rounds to leave a note and sign off.

## Being And Becoming Excellent - Reflections

*We got to Room 813 of the MICU where JG was staying at 11:17, and as we were entering, two family members immediately left with their heads bowed. A nurse informed us immediately that "he expired at 11:02." I felt a sudden wave of emotions. First was the obvious grief from the first death of a patient while under my "care." I've had patients who I was following pass away later after I chart-stalked them. But I have never seen one of them dead in front of me. I'll never forget the look of JG, with his distinct color and the picture of Jesus on his bed. I then felt immense guilt for previously having been so focused on thinking of the pathophysiology of his disease rather than on the person himself, and how I was so selfish that I had even begun to think it was good that he was too unstable to get an MRI and EEG so that I could see another patient. And then I felt the guilt of how I didn't feel particularly drawn to him when he was alive, but suddenly, I felt all this emotion now that he had passed away.*

*After he passed, some members of our team expressed how sad it was that he had passed. But then, back in our rounding room, a physician said that we were going to remove him from our list because, "well, he's dead." It was so nonchalant and without emotion! I remember thinking how crude it was to think like that. But was I any better when I was having such selfish thoughts when the patient was alive?*

*I don't know what my point is in sharing this story and writing this as my paper. I guess part of it is that I didn't have many people to talk to about this. I talked to my brother, who is also in medical school, about it, and he helped reaffirm my emotions, but he didn't have any good emotions. Someone completely removed from the medicine had asked me previously how I cope with sadness when it comes to patients. And, I feel like, at least acutely, you just must repress the emotions to be able to get through your day. In a sense, I wonder if it is almost necessary to become a little jaded emotionally to be a good physician.*

> *Now that I reflect on how I felt when first seeing JG, I hate the way I thought and how selfish I was. I'm so disappointed that I got to that point and hope to never feel like that again. I also hope that I never forget how bad I felt when I saw JG that last time. It'll be a reminder for me that I have such a unique opportunity to touch lives at their most desperate moment. At the same time, I hope that I never have to feel that again, because it was miserable. However, for that to happen, I feel like it is necessary to become numb to that emotion or to at least be able to repress it to a manageable level.*

JW's experience reminds us of our fundamental human nature—physical, mental, emotional, and spiritual—with our potential for goodness and kindness toward self and the other, our potential to be not-so-good and even downright selfish. What we are and what we become is in large measure what we choose to be and to become. Most of us have had experiences like JW's.

We are physical, finite living beings, each in a physical world that most of us can see, feel, hear, touch, taste, smell, and take for granted. We develop physically, mentally, emotionally, and spiritually from birth to death. The reality is, that as we live, we are also slowly dying, until that final breath when we experience death. The problem is: We are sentient beings, capable of self-reflection, and we are aware of our finite nature and its limitations, and of the terrifying truth that we will die.

These truths are well exemplified in JW's reflection. It is clear that he was shocked to suddenly see JG "dead," physically dead. He experienced an immediate "wave of emotions" that he had not felt before. Although he had known other patients whom he had "chart stalked" and who had died, he had never actually been in a room with a dead patient. JW comes face to face with death, most likely projecting empathetically and unconsciously about his own death. The finality of this event for JW produced feelings of guilt and insecurity. He was regretful of his earlier thoughts about and reactions to JG's condition. His subsequent feelings of sadness, grief, selfishness, then guilt are all normal psychological reactions.

## Being And Becoming Excellent - Reflections

If we live long enough, we eventually become aware of the stark reality of death, at least to one degree or another. Unconsciously, this truth is so terrifying that we repress it and seek security and protection from it by projection—onto someone or something that we believe gives us the security and protection we seek; pick your something or someone. From a psychoanalytic perspective, we know these projections are necessary for survival, but they are only illusions, or hero myths, which ultimately fail.

Upon review of JW's reflection, it appears that how JW processed this reality was less than optimal. He dealt with the situation alone, except for superficially talking to his brother. He self-identified the need to repress his feelings. This is less than optimal for personal as well as professional growth in maintaining resiliency while dealing with suffering and death. Unfortunately, this kind of experience is more common than we like to admit. However, medical schools and healthcare systems are beginning to address the need for support at times like these through a more structured grieving process, along with medical ethics education and training. JW did not receive this positive approach. Instead of taking the opportunity to have an immediate open dialogue in a safe, non-threatening space, the physician in charge simply and nonchalantly indicated that JG would be taken off their list because, "Well, he's dead." This non-compassionate dynamic explains JW's reaction and difficulty in resolving very conflicted feelings and emotions.

Recall SP in the second case above. She had a similar experience of witnessing a dead patient, but unlike JW, she did not have to deal with the emotional trauma alone. She had an experienced surgeon mentor who intentionally and compassionately guided and helped her navigate through the difficult experience as it happened and then again during the post-traumatic period. By participating in a positive debriefing process with a professional experienced in dealing with post-traumatic stress, she was able to deal with her feelings and emotions adequately, recognizing their legitimacy and working through them to a level of acceptance and understanding that increases future resiliency and avoiding unhealthy repressions.

In conclusion, the relationality-responsibility ethic seems to best address how we should behave. No set of rules and regulations can completely answer how we should act in every situation of suffering. No end goal or mandate is so compelling that any means to obtain it is justified. Each human being brings a certain developmental history, family dynamic, geography, and culture, along with a religious or non-religious faith and set of mores. These may change with time and circumstances. The relationality-responsibility ethic embraces openness, awareness of diversity and differences, and increased sensitivity and respect for difference. It recognizes our common humanity, which leads to wisdom and understanding. With these understandings comes the realization that "just like me," the other shares the same needs for food, clothing, shelter, intimate and nurturing relationships (family, friends, community), and a certain level of flourishing. We know that we are neurologically hardwired for empathy. Empathy naturally leads to compassion, i.e., the motivation to help another in need. In Reflection 6, we will address the science behind these ideas. What is compassion? And does love have anything to do with it? What is love? This is where science, theology, and Spirit intersect.

## Reflection 6—Love and Compassion

*Love*

> *If I speak in the tongues of mortals and of angels, but do not have love, I am a noisy gong or a clanging cymbal. And if I have prophetic powers, and understand all mysteries and all knowledge, and if I have all faith, to remove mountains, but do not have love, I am nothing. If I give away all my possessions, and if I hand over my body so that I may boast, but do not have love, I gain nothing. Love is patient; love is kind; love is not envious or boastful or arrogant or rude. It does not insist on its own way; it is not irritable or resentful; it does not rejoice in wrongdoing but rejoices in the truth. It bears all things, believes all things, hopes all things, endures all things. Love never ends. But as for prophecies, they will come to an end; as for tongues, they will cease; as for knowledge, it will come to an end. For we know only in part, and we prophesy only in part; but when the complete comes, the partial will come to an end. When I was a child, I spoke like a child, I thought like a child, I reasoned like a child; when I became an adult, I put an end to childish ways. For now, we see in a mirror, dimly, but then we will see face to face. Now I know only in part; then I will know fully, even as I have been fully known. And now faith, hope, and love abide, these three; and the greatest of these is love. —Paul of Tarsus to the Corinthians (c. 53-54 CE)*

I have been attending monthly "Filosophs" meetings now for over ten years. Here is a group of eight to ten men who have developed a special relationship with each other individually and as a group. Open, committed to seeking the truth, eclectic in interests and spiritual persuasion, we have come from all kinds of backgrounds—a lawyer, several medical doctors, an artist, a businessman; some religious, some not—but all philosophers, "lovers of wisdom," seeking truth.

One meeting I will never forget. We gathered to talk about values and how they play in the human story. Our spouses and significant others were invited to join us. In the comfort and safety of his home, the evening facilitator gave us a list of some twenty-five to thirty values that are commonly expressed. Each of us was to select the fifteen that we felt were most important or meaningful to us.

After a period, we were then asked if we would like to share the ones we chose. Several did. After that, we were asked to choose the top ten, then the top five, each time allowing time to share for those who wished to do so. Following this exercise, we began a lively discussion of why values, individual and societal, were important. After some discussion, I was inspired to ask the group to individually write down the value that was number one on their list. Without exception, the winner was *love*. Interesting...

So, let's begin this Reflection with the idea of love. What do we mean when we use the word? The English term, by itself without explanation or context, is fraught with ambiguity. When asked about it, we rightfully should ask, "Which kind are you talking about?" Ancient Greeks granulated the concept by using different words when describing different kinds of love: Libido and *Eros* for erotic, sexual, passionate love; *philia* for friendship or brotherly love; *storge* for familial love, such as between parents and their children, implying a kind of dependency; and *agape* love for universal, unconditional "God" love. Psychologists today draw several other kinds of love from Greek writings that seem to complete the list: *ludus* for a playful, uncommitted love with a focus on fun, perhaps conquest, no strings attached; *pragma* for a practical love based on duty and long-term interests (e.g., arranged relationships); and *philau a* for self-love, which can be healthy or unhealthy (i.e., hubris).[58]

"There have been many definitions of the term "love." When searching for a definition online, there were almost two billion listings (I did not check them all!). The definitions at the top of the list were "an intense feeling of deep affection for someone or something" and "a great interest and pleasure in something," and for the verb, "to feel a deep romantic or sexual attachment to (someone)." However, I believe these definitions fall severely short and fail to capture love as a primary irreducible value and motivator for life and relationships.

In his short 1963 exposition *Morality and Beyond*, Paul Tillich gives a compelling and impelling argument for what he describes as the moral imperative. The premise is that humans must be and become persons in relationships with other persons in a community. He argues that the moral imperative for each of us is "the demand that one becomes actually what one is, both essentially and potentially. It is the power of a man's being, given to him by nature, which he shall actualize in time and space. His true being shall become his actual being—this is the moral imperative." He goes on to say, "And since his true being is the being of a person in a community of persons, the moral imperative has this content: to become a person. Every moral act is an act in which an individual self establishes himself or herself as a person."[59]

I agree with Tillich. Life demands that we become a person in a relationship with other persons in a community. Implied in being a person are all those accumulated life experiences between birth and death that make us the person we are now and the person we will become. These raise questions: What is the optimal personhood that we should become? What is it that motivates us to become that person?

I believe Tillich would answer the first question by saying that obligatory to personhood is being and becoming a moral person. He admits some persons are amoral. Amorality, simply put, is "having or showing no concern [or sense] about whether behavior is morally right or wrong, being neither moral nor immoral."[60] For example, a fish or other non-sentient being would be seen as amoral. Scentific methodology embraces amorality as one of its guiding principles.

Tillich would likely answer the second question by saying that love is what motivates us to be moral persons. Although he gives a good account of the necessity and motivating power of legalism, i.e., of rules and regulations, he concludes these are insufficient and ultimately fail to lead to a truly moral person. It is love that fulfills the intent of the law and that ultimately leads to a truly moral person.

Tillich goes on to explain his concept of love by saying that love is by its very nature internal to the person. Love "grasps" the person as being of ultimate concern. Tillich writes, "The desire for union of the separated (which is ultimately *re*-union) is love."[61] The principle of justice is inherent in love and cannot be separated from it, although justice can be expressed externally with detachment and little involvement. Love expresses justice from its internal being, from its communion, and a deeper level of involvement and participation with the other, recognizing the other as an equal person in every sense of being a person. Thus, "love becomes the ultimate moral principle, including justice and transcending it at the same time."[62] Justice is not lessened, but increased; it becomes creative in the sense that it judges, forgives, reconciles, and restores all at the same time. It is inherent in unconditional love, a love described by Tillich and others, including me, as "agape" love.

I agree with Tillich that love is a complex of different qualities or elements, all-natural and simultaneously dynamic in expression, with agape as the self-transcendent quality, that quality that expresses the ultimate religious element in love. Remember, Tillich, defines "religion" as "being grasped by an ultimate concern." Thus, according to this definition, every person is naturally "religious," with love at the center of that person's being. Here, parenthetically, one may recall my reflection (Reflection 1) on Monod's work. Monod, rightfully or wrongfully, concludes that the principle of invariance (the reproductive mandate) precedes teleonomy (purpose) as the natural basic life force, a force requiring the *literal* union of the separated. So, in the true sense of the concept, invariance is the libido-eros element of love.

To this latter point, Tillich continues,

>"Agape as the self-transcending element of love is not separated from the other elements [qualities] that usually are described as epithymia—the libido quality of love, philia—the friendship quality of love, and eros—the mystical quality of love. In all of them, what we have called "the urge toward the re-union of the separated" is effective, and all of them stand under the judgment of agape. For love is one, even if one of its qualities predominates. None

*of the qualities is ever completely absent. There is, for example, the compassion element of philia and eros in agape, and there is the agape quality in genuine compassion (a fact important for dialogue between Christianity and Buddhism). It is this agape element that prevents participation in the other one from becoming mere identification with him, as compassion prevents agape from becoming a detached act of mere obedience to the "law of love." And there is eros in agape, and agape in eros, a fact that permitted Christianity to receive into itself the eros-created classical culture, both rational and mystical. It is the agape element in eros that prevents culture from becoming a non-serious, merely transitory entertainment, just as eros prevents agape from becoming a moralistic turning away from the creative potentialities in nature and man toward an exclusive commitment to a God who can only be feared or obeyed, but not loved. For without eros toward the ultimate good there is no love toward God. Even the libidinous quality of love is always present in the highest form of eros, philia, and agape. Man is a multidimensional unity and not a composite of parts. Therefore, all elements of man's being participate in every moral decision and action."[63]*

Thus, love in all its forms and complexity is at the center of our being and is the primary motivator of all our actions in the community—from the acquisition of our most basic physical needs to our natural pro-creative actions to our most transcendent actions—all valid expressions of life as human beings. The moral imperative demands we strive to become loving persons in the community. This, in turn, requires a deeper understanding of this central complex motivator called love and of *agape* as the overriding quality necessary to becoming a moral person in communion with other persons, i.e., to become excellent.

Finally, Tillich brings into sharp focus the ethics (behaviors) of the moral imperative. He summarizes three types of ethics, what he calls "solutions," that historically have been presented and embraced over the centuries. He argues that none of these "solutions" or "types of ethics" have satisfied the moral requirement. He summarizes in a somewhat different language what we have already described in the previous reflections.

He first describes the static *supernaturalistic* solution, represented by the Roman Catholic Church and expressed in the ethics of Thomas Aquinas, which is based on Aristotelian philosophy and a combination of doctrines, laws, and Magisterium rules and regulations. Second, he describes the *dynamic-naturalistic-progressive* the solution, represented by the National Socialism movement and expressed in the ethics of the humanistic philosophers of life. In a paper in 2000, D-Vasilescu describes, "Tillich knew that, through Nazism (i.e., National Socialism), socialism degenerated into a false [prophecy], because through nationalism and racism, socialism became idolatry," which is an excessively strong "ism" that led to the tragic holocaust of Nazi Germany with the complicity of the German Christian Church[64][65]

Third, he describes the *rationalistic-progressive* solution, based on Anglo-Saxon common sense, which expresses the ethics of the philosophers of reason (Kant, Bentham, Mill, Fletcher, et al).[66] He concludes that none of these satisfy our current need in this increasingly complex time and space. Tillich argues that only love in all its forms can satisfy our current needs. I would rephrase, "Only love in all its forms in the context of the relationality-responsibility ethic can satisfy our current need."

If these thoughts and reflections are compelling, then all beg the question, "How?" How do we love with true excellence? I believe the value of compassion provides a partial answer: We love most excellently when we love with compassion.

### *Compassion*

> "The principle of compassion lies at the heart of all religious, ethical, and spiritual traditions, calling us always to treat all others as we wish to be treated ourselves. Compassion impels us to work tirelessly to alleviate the suffering of our fellow creatures, to dethrone ourselves from the center of our world and put another there and to honor the inviolable sanctity of every single human being, treating everybody, without exception, with absolute justice, equity, and respect."[67]—*Excerpt from The Charter for Compassion*

The international Charter for Compassion best expresses compassion as the motivating value/principle that in large measure answers the question, "How do we love?" We act with love and compassion because we are motivated by the value of love and compassion. They are inseparable. They constitute the two sides of the same coin.

I first understood the term "compassion" as both a noun and a verb. However, the concept is much more complex than it first appears.[68] Compassion can be defined as noticing the suffering of self or the other, the desire to do something to relieve the suffering, and the commitment to act. However, compassion is not the actual action itself. To be optimally beneficial, the action taken must be based on wisdom and discernment of the situation and circumstances. Otherwise, unintended adverse consequences may result. So, one can view compassion as essentially a three-step motivation process, and the separate action taken is one based on a wisdom and discernment process.

Compassion is definitely a call to action to relieve suffering. It requires great courage and strength. For example, consider the compassionate action taken by non-Jews in Nazi-controlled Europe during World War II. Many took a great risk in protecting and safe-harboring Jewish families during this period. Such action argues against the currently popular belief that compassion is "soft," non-effective, and not realistic. There are many other examples of how such a love/compassion ethic brings about the relief of suffering and even fosters flourishing in our day-to-day lives in the community—in our homes, at work, and in our neighborhoods. To this definition of compassion, I might add "with loving kindness." It is possible to act compassionately and show very little loving-kindness. This complex of love and compassion with loving kindness is a perfect example of the relationality-responsibility ethic.

The science of compassion also suggests that empathy is required if you are to be truly compassionate, so I would like to reflect a bit on empathy. Empathy means resonating with the thoughts, feelings, emotions, and situation of another. Two components make up empathy, cognitive and affective. Cognitive empathy originates from the higher brain centers and enables us to acquire knowledge and understanding of the situation of another, while affective empathy enables us to resonate emotionally with the emotions of another. Both are necessary for empathy to lead to compassion. The cognitive component allows for awareness and recognition of pain or suffering, while the affective component inspires us to act. A popular comprehensive compassion cultivation training program, Compassion Integrity Training (CIT), calls the combination of components "empathic concern—the ability to understand the emotions, thoughts, and motivations of another and to resonate with them."[69] In layman's terms, one looks at empathy as the ability to put oneself in the shoes of the other. But empathy is far more complex than we might first think. It does not necessarily lead to the good of all humanity.

Scientific evidence indicates that we are "hardwired" for empathy, if for no other reason than for our own individual and human species' survival and level of flourishing. If this is true, then we can see, for example, why the German people turned inward and embraced the promises of Adolf Hitler. They empathized internally with each other as a result of the pain and suffering after World War I when no other country came to their aid. Adolf Hitler promised a new nation, strong and resilient against the rest of the world. They put their trust, obedience, and future solely in his hands. And of course, we know the horrific outcomes of that decision, never to be forgotten and hopefully never to be repeated. And yes, we still have this kind of potentially negative empathic concern in our world, a reality and truth we must recognize and be vigilant to avoid.

There is another aspect of empathy that is even more complicated, one that must be considered, i.e., empathic distress. Some call it burnout. Many mislabel this condition as "compassion fatigue," but this is a misnomer. The generally accepted definition of compassion used in many scientific and healthcare studies is awareness of the suffering of another, desire to relieve or mitigate that suffering, and commitment to action to provide relief with loving kindness. This definition precludes equating compassion with empathy. Empathy is only one step toward compassion and compassionate action. Empathic distress is "self-focused." Empathic concern is "other focused." Empathic distress is the feeling of being overwhelmed by what you perceive as too much suffering for one individual to do anything to relieve it.

We have little difficulty in feeling empathy for one other person's suffering, and certainly, if the suffering is being experienced by a member of our close family or circle. It becomes more difficult as the suffering increases both in time and amount or beyond our closest circles. We see this after natural disasters and in long-term care in the healthcare field. Being aware of this aspect of empathy is important. Empathic distress is a reality, and when we recognize and become aware that we are experiencing it, then we are better prepared to refrain from judging ourselves too harshly. We are also better prepared to accept a situation with equanimity and to act in some measure to relieve the suffering. Note: The suffering may be our own.

Another partial answer to the question, "How do we love?" seems to lie within what we mean by "sympathetic joy," i.e., empathy for another's joy. A loving person is a person who not only recognizes the suffering of the other and does something to relieve it, but also is one who celebrates the joys of the other. But our human nature is such that our ego and self-centeredness often lead to envy or jealousy for the other's success or good fortune, rather than appreciating and sharing their joy. To express sympathetic joy requires intention, and humility which implies a degree of empathy, which we have seen is a necessary but insufficient element for compassion and sympathetic joy.[70]

Another partial, and important answer to the question, "How do we love?" must include an understanding of what is meant by "circles of compassion." One needs only look at the case of oneself. It is easier for me to be compassionate and share the sympathetic joy with those closest to me, with my family and friends. We may be able to extend compassion to close neighbors, to the local community, state, and nation, although it is more difficult with these. It is harder when we attempt to extend the circle of compassion to other neighborhoods, other groups, other communities, states, and nations. We might even say that it is impossible to extend compassion and sympathetic joy to the entire world. But I would argue, as many do, that our human survival depends on our being able to step outside ourselves and our closest circles and extend compassion to the entire world, taking what I call "a view at 35,000 feet." If this is true, we humans have a lot of work ahead.

Finally, recent scientific research in the healthcare field shows that compassion matters for health and well-being, and that it can be learned and cultivated, but we must desire to be more compassionate to self, to others, and the world if such education and training is to be effective. In their recently published book *Compassionomics: The Revolutionary Scientific Evidence that Compassion Makes a Difference*, authors, researchers, and physicians Stephen Trzeciak and Anthony Mazzarelli present compelling evidence for the foregoing conclusions.[71] Compassion does make a difference in healthcare systems and can be learned. They conducted a comprehensive, complex review of the healthcare research literature on the impact of compassion or the lack thereof on the healthcare system and its stakeholders, which includes the entire human community. These results have startling implications, not just in the healthcare system, but in all human social systems. We need to be more compassionate. Our human survival depends on it.

## Being And Becoming Excellent - Reflections

*"If you want to be happy, practice compassion. If you want others to be happy, practice compassion."* —His Holiness, the 14th Dalai Lama

## Reflection 7—Forgiveness, Reconciliation, and Restoration

As Commanding Officer of Naval Health Clinic Hawaii during the period 2004 – 2007, I was obligated by higher medical department policies to medically support deployments of the U.S. Marine Corps Third Regiment stationed at Kaneohe Bay, Hawaii, with hospital corpsmen from my command, corpsmen who were trained for combat. Hospital Corpsman Ben M was assigned to my command. Conscientious, dedicated, and committed, Ben was a good sailor, a good corpsman, and well-trained as an NEC 8404 Hospital Corpsman, the designation of specialty training for missions with the U.S. Marines. Along with another ten to fifteen hospital corpsmen, I temporarily assigned Ben to accompany the Marines to Iraq/Afghanistan on one of their deployments in 2005. .

Soon after entering the combat theater, Ben experienced a tragic improvised explosive device (IED) incident, in which one Marine was killed and several others seriously injured. Ben was the sole corpsman on the scene. Ben, fortunately, was not injured physically, but he suffered a psychological injury, which proved serious and lasting for him. Soon after returning from deployment to Naval Health Clinic Hawaii, he began developing increasing signs of post-traumatic stress disorder (PTSD). One of my policies as "Skipper" was to have each corpsman returning from deployment write at least a one-page summary of their deployment with reflections. Each would come to my office, and we would review and discuss his report and reflections. It seemed for many a useful re-integrating experience. So, I knew early on that Ben had been involved in serious trauma and that he felt he had not done enough at the scene, that he had been inadequate in the situation.

Ben began seeing a psychiatrist and began counseling at Tripler Army Medical Center (TAMC). Our command chaplain engaged with Ben, supporting his spiritual needs. We noticed he was having increasing difficulties with his duties at the health clinic and in his relationships, specifically with his girlfriend. Soon, he was hospitalized at TAMC. I made several personal visits to see him and spent some quality time encouraging him in his care, focusing mostly on the emotional/spiritual impact on him. I was also in close touch with his girlfriend, who was also in close contact with Ben's psychiatrist. You could say we were an official unofficial team caring for Ben. One evening after arriving home and just before retiring, I received a phone call from Ben's girlfriend. Ben had left Hawaii on a commercial airplane and gone back to the U.S. mainland. She had the name of the airline and the flight number. If this was true, Ben had gone AWOL, absent without leave, from the command. That was a serious military offense. It was up to me as commanding officer to officially respond. Given Ben's mental condition, I was not willing to strictly apply The Uniform Code of Military Justice (UCMJ), the military's justice system of criminal offenses under military law. I called his psychiatrist, who again reiterated the seriousness of his medical/mental condition. We agreed our response had to be one of compassion and what I call "tough love." The goal was to get Ben back to the command, where we could handle the situation directly, legally, and most important, medically.

We discovered from his girlfriend that Ben was most likely heading to the home of a family or friend in Florida. His flight itinerary indicated that he would be landing in Pensacola, Florida. The Navy has a training air station in Pensacola with an associated naval hospital not far from the base. I knew the commanding officer of the hospital, who was also a personal friend. I called him and explained the situation. He agreed. I did not want Ben arrested and incarcerated, but rather intercepted at the airport and admitted to the hospital for evaluation by psychiatry. I would send one of my staff hospital corpsmen to escort him back to Hawaii to be hospitalized for further psychiatric evaluation and treatment.

*Miraculously, the plan worked. I had one surprised sailor when he landed in Pensacola. Ben was admitted to Naval Hospital Pensacola. The hospital corpsman I had sent arrived and then escorted him back to Hawaii. Within twenty-four hours, Ben was back to TAMC, where he was admitted by his regular psychiatrist and received the care he needed. The plan resulted in Ben completing his short remaining military obligation with an honorable discharge from the U.S. Navy. Ben has periodically kept in touch over the years, deeply appreciative of how his "Skipper" took care of him. And I am deeply grateful for how I was moved to handle the situation the way we did. Moved by Grace is the only explanation I have....*

I am convinced that only with the values of love and compassion and with the process of forgiveness, reconciliation, and restoration can there be true peace and healing of self, of others, and of the world. The story of Ben is just one example that supports this truth. Our nature is one of physical, mental, emotional, and spiritual potential in which we may find ourselves dynamically anywhere within each domain. The truth of love and compassion exists throughout our nature. Although individually we are separated from each other by physical reality, each of us shares common humanity: the striving to meet needs and desires, to be happy, and to avoid suffering and pain. We are driven to connect at some level with one another by the various forms of love described earlier. Furthermore, many believe, as do I, that there is a universal Spirit that inspires and even compels us to desire these connections. However, the reality of separation and our individual survival ego and tendency to self-centeredness can naturally lead to a lack of heedfulness about not harming. So, we harm and cause suffering to ourselves, to others, and the environment. Thus, forgiveness, reconciliation, and restoration are required if we are to move toward a more loving and compassionate world in which true peace and healing for the individual and community are realized.

In November 2019, a conference entitled "Mind and Life Conversations on Compassion, Interconnection and Transformation" was held in Dharamsala, India, where Tenzin Gyatso, the 14$^{th}$ Dalai Lama, resides. His Holiness was joined by world authorities and researchers in the science of compassion. For the conversations, he was joined by well-known psychologist Pumla Gobodo Madikizela from South Africa. The dialogue between His Holiness and Pumla was powerful in its depth and understanding of compassion. The discussion provided significant insight to me as to why we need a process of forgiveness, reconciliation, and restoration.[72]

Pumla had sat on the Truth and Reconciliation Commission with Bishop Desmond Tutu. This was a commission authorized by South Africa's President Nelson Mandela post-apartheid to bring victims and perpetrators together voluntarily to foster reconciliation and restoration. Confession, truth-telling, compassion, and forgiveness were integral to the level of success achieved by the commission. Pumla had the opportunity to interview several female victims who were willing to forgive the killing of their male spouses. Through these interviews, she was able to get to know Eugene de Kock, considered "the most brutal of apartheid's covert police operatives," who was well-known as "Prime Evil."

She published an account of her experience in 2006.[73] Early in the account, she poignantly reflected on her first interview with de Kock,

> *"I had seen his other side, where I had shared a common idiom of humanity with him [touching his hand], and I needed to find out how and why it had been silenced [within me]. By the time I met de Kock again, I was ready to see reality as it had been revealed to me: two sides of de Kock, one evil, and the other—the one I was more afraid of confronting—a human being capable of feeling, crying, and knowing pain."[74]*

Touching de Kock's hand at the end of an earlier interview was a significant event for Pumla. She shared this insight:

*"That moment back in the interview room gave me a glimpse of what he could have been. Hard as the memory of having touched him was, the experience made me realize something I probably was not*

*prepared for—that good and evil exist in our lives, and that evil, like good, is always a possibility. And that was what frightened me."*[75]

Later she reflected on a subsequent interview, giving one the sense of depth and complexity that can be involved in the forgiveness and reconciliation process:

*"I looked at his hands for the first time, my eyes focusing on the left hand, the one I had touched, half expecting to see some peculiar features in it. But I did not. As if he was aware of my new interest in his hands, de Kock placed them squarely on the table to balance himself as he sat down. His fingernails were surprisingly neatly manicured. The nails were clean and white, with tidy symmetrical edges. One might even have been persuaded to call his hands beautiful. They could easily have been those of a friend or colleague. For a moment, it struck me that the line separating good and evil is paper-thin".*

Upon viewing the video of the conversation between His Holiness and Pumla, my "Aha" moment came when I realized what "compassion" means in two quite different cultural settings—the Indian/Tibetan culture of the Dalai Lama and the South Africa/apartheid culture of Pumla. As is evident from the above quotes and reflections, Pumla comes from a culture historically steeped in stark racism, inequity, hate, and unabashed killings of those opposed to the white apartheid government. His Holiness comes from a culture where compassion is cultivated from the beginning—in infancy.

During the Dharamsala conversations, when confronted with the idea of compassion as the key to the ills of humanity, Pumla acknowledged the truth of this statement from His Holiness, but respectfully excepted that in places like South Africa, compassion cannot be realistic, normative operative value for that culture, at least not yet; but rather, the values and actions of forgiveness, reconciliation, and restoration must take precedence over cultivating compassion if such a contrasting norm and training is to be desired and effectively embodied in a culture like that. Although not the end-all solution to the evils of apartheid, Mandela's post-apartheid Truth and Reconciliation Commission work has made tremendous steps forward. We might say that South Africa has become a more compassionate South Africa. Is it possible to envision a long-range reality in which compassion is the norm and compassion cultivation the standard from cradle to grave in South Africa? I am an optimist. I think so.

In comparison, when I reflect on the value of compassion in Tibetan culture, it appears that compassion is already normative from birth to death. The Dalai Lama himself was raised in this culture where compassion, with the Golden Rule as the guiding principle, is cultivated lifelong. As an infant and young child, he was immersed in this culture and tradition that enthroned him at age five, when the 14th Dalai Lama believed that he was the reincarnation of the 13th Dalai Lama. At least for me, this explains why His Holiness emphasizes compassion-cultivation training from birth as a key solution to the ills of humanity. One of his famous sayings points to this: "Compassion is the radicalism of our time." For him, compassion is our true self and should be recognized and cultivated. His love of science, his alliance with well-known and respected research centers, and his Social-Emotional-Ethics Learning program (SEE Learning) are current witnesses to the Tibetan ethical stance.[76]

In conclusion, it seems to me obvious that to transform humanity and the global culture from a normative individualistic, self-centered mindset with a high risk of harming to a normative individual-community mindset of compassionate other-centeredness leading to well-being and flourishing, then the processes of forgiveness, reconciliation, and restoration are necessary in the current state of the world.

This leads me to my final reflection, Reflection 8.

Being And Becoming Excellent - Reflections

## Reflection 8—The Path to True Peace and Healing
### The Most Excellent Way

*The Charter for COMPASSION[77]*

The principle of compassion lies at the heart of all religious, ethical, and spiritual traditions, calling us always to treat all others as we wish to be treated ourselves. Compassion impels us to work tirelessly to alleviate the suffering of our fellow creatures, to dethrone ourselves from the center of our world and put another there, and to honor the inviolable sanctity of every single human being, treating everybody, without exception, with absolute justice, equity, and respect.

It is also necessary for both public and private life to refrain consistently and empathically from inflicting pain. To act or speak violently out of spite, chauvinism, or self-interest, to impoverish, exploit or deny basic rights to anybody, and to incite hatred by denigrating others—even our enemies—is a denial of our common humanity. We acknowledge that we have failed to live compassionately and that some have even increased the sum of human misery in the name of religion.

We hereby call upon all men and women:

To restore compassion to the center of morality and religion
To return to the ancient principle that any interpretation of scripture that breeds violence, hatred, or disdain is illegitimate

*To ensure that youth are given accurate and respectful information about other traditions, religions, and cultures*
*To encourage a positive appreciation of cultural and religious diversity*
*To cultivate an informed empathy with the suffering of all human beings—even those regarded as enemies*

*We urgently need to make compassion a clear, luminous, and dynamic force in our polarized world. Rooted in a principled determination to transcend selfishness, compassion can break down political, dogmatic, ideological, and religious boundaries. Born of our deep interdependence, compassion is essential to human relationships and to a fulfilled humanity. It is the path to enlightenment and indispensable to the creation of a just economy and a peaceful global community.*

One of the first questions I am asked by those who believe they are already compassionate but desire to be more compassionate, and who have affirmed the Charter for Compassion is, "So, what's next?" I usually respond, "I recommend learning what compassion means." For one thing, compassion is not pity. It is not feeling sorry for yourself or someone else. The fact is, every person, organization, and city government believes it is compassionate. Even so, I sense they do not understand what compassion is. Many think compassion is "soft," a sign of weakness, and that expressing compassion is like asking to be run over, to be a doormat.

This doubt about my understanding of compassion comes into clear focus when I think about my lesser thoughts, feelings, and actions when I am driving on a busy, crowded expressway in Dallas during rush hours. When I look in the mirror at myself in the morning, I realize that there are many situations like this in which I could be more compassionate. I want to be more compassionate. So how does a person, an organization, or a community learn what compassion is, and how do we become more compassionate? I am convinced that it is only through intentional education and compassion cultivation training that one truly can know, embody, and express compassion at the deepest level. You gotta want it, and more of it!

If you are just beginning the journey toward more intentional compassion, I suggest a personal or group study of Karen Armstrong's *Twelve Steps to a Compassionate Life*. There are many other good books on compassion, almost too numerous to count. There are also many programs available for learning and embodying compassion, from pre-K to age "105." The list is long, but you might start at the Charter for Compassion's Compassion Education Institute (CEI),[78] where there are multiple offerings. I have taken several, and they are quite good. Affirming the Charter for Compassion was an early first step for me in my journey. Engaging in the Charter's work has been a real positive influence on my life journey and understanding of compassion as a core common human value. Nurturing compassion at all phases of life are key. It must begin early in life through good parental support and guidance. And it must continue throughout life.

The Charter currently embraces several already established, independent programs. ThinkEqual, for pre-K children, is specifically designed for ages 3-6.[79] For the K-12 level, a recently published Social, Emotional, and Ethical (SEE) Learning Program developed at Emory University is quite good.[80] And for adults eighteen and older, there are several comprehensive compassion-cultivation programs. Compassion Cultivation Training[81] (CCT) developed at Stanford University, Cognitive-Based Compassion Training[82] (CBCT) developed at Emory University, and Compassion Integrity Training[83] (CIT) developed at Life University in Atlanta, Georgia, are the better-known programs. Any one of these would be a good choice. The Charter has embraced and is engaged with Compassion Integrity Training. I have taken CCT and CIT and am currently a CIT Facilitator. Since I am most familiar with CIT, I would like to describe and reflect more deeply on that program.

I appreciate the pedagogy of CIT, the three levels of understanding from head to heart to hands (receiving new knowledge, making it personal with critical insight through exercises and practices to "aha" moments. I appreciate progressing toward embodiment through "practice, practice, practice," which is the ultimate aim of the program to ensure that compassion becomes an internal and integral part of who you are. It works.

## Being And Becoming Excellent - Reflections

The curriculum is divided into three series and ten skills.[84] Although flexible schedules are possible, the usual course is once weekly over ten weeks, two hours each week, in person. The first series of four skills focus on the self and is entitled "Self-Compassion." It is a well-known fact that in the Western world, being self-compassionate is almost an anathema, regardless of gender. "I can do it. I am tough. I can take it. I can pick myself up by my bootstraps and carry on. I do not need to be compassionate to myself. It's enough to be compassionate to others. I am in control." Sound familiar? The fact is, unless we learn how to be compassionate to ourselves and embody that level of compassion, we will have a really hard time being compassionate to others, especially those who are beyond our close circle.

Series 1 skills include: "Calming the Body and Mind," " Ethical Mindfulness," "Emotional Awareness," and finally "Self-Compassion." Each skill builds on the previous one, so it is important to cover each step along the journey.

Series 2 topic is "Relating to Others," and it consists of the next four skills: "Impartiality and Common Humanity," "Forgiveness and Gratitude," "Empathic Concern," and "Compassion." The learning outcome aims not only to solidify our closest circle of compassion, but also to expand our compassion to larger and larger circles of compassion that will include neighbors, community, state, nation, and the world, and even those we consider "enemy." It is possible. I encourage you to refer back to Pumla's experience with de Koch. As already stated, each skill builds upon the previous one; likewise, each series of skills builds on the previous series.

Series 3 of CIT skills is unique among the comprehensive compassion training programs, and it was a definite "draw" for me. Entitled "Engaging in Systems," the third series addresses our relationship with systems, which could be as close as our family system or as disparate as a large organization in the corporate world, be it in arts, business, education, environment, healthcare, government, or other nongovernmental, nonprofit organizations, just to give a few examples. How do I as an individual within an interest group decide how best to change or transform a system without causing unintended negative consequences?

CIT promotes two important skills in this series, "Appreciating Interdependence" and "Engaging with Discernment," which enable compassionate transformation. Here, CIT introduces a beautiful metaphor—a great white owl, flying with wings outstretched. One wing represents compassion as the motivation for action; the other wing represents discernment as the wisdom needed to make optimal, compassionate decisions. Obviously, transformation in large systems is complex, requiring time, energy, great patience, resilience, and equanimity.

We have already described such complexity in the transformation of South Africa from what it was to what it is becoming. Ireland is another similar example. These kinds of transformations required the deep embodiment of compassion expressed by Nelson Mandela during his many years of imprisonment, and also in the compassionate actions he took upon election as President, such as establishing the Truth and Reconciliation Commission. Although we may not be Nelson Mandela, we can do similarly in whatever system we find ourselves in and however small we think the action is. As my mom used to tell me when I was a kid, "It is the pennies that make the dollars, so gather and save your pennies." Each of us doing our small part as just one "penny" (engaging in compassionate action) can along with many other "pennies" (compassionate actions) transform the world, a very worthy adventure. Please join me on that journey! Godspeed!

# End Notes

## Prologue

[2] *Interesting language/scripture found in John 16:12-13a. Some theologians refer to the "Spirit of truth/He" as "Lady Wisdom/She," expressed indirectly in the Genesis stories of the Hebrew bible describing creation. Some might prefer to interpret the pronoun as non-gender, "I am."*

[3] *Reucroft, Steven. Northeastern University. "What Exactly Is the Higgs Boson?" Scientific American. https://www.scientificamerican.com/article/what-exactly-is-the-higgs/ cited 16 May 2020.*

[4] *Carroll, Sean. The Particle at the End of the Universe.*

[5] *Chalmers, David. 2014 TED Talk "How do you Explain Consciousness". Cited 16 May2020.https://www.ted.com/talks/david_chalmers_how_do_you_explain_consciousness/discussion?langugae=e n#t-73764.*

## Introduction

[6] *Tobolowsky, Paul. Stardust Dancing: A Seeker's Guide to the Miraculous. Charleston: Create Space, 2013.*

[7] *Curran, Charles E. The Catholic Moral Tradition Today: A Synthesis. Washington DC: Georgetown University Press. 1999.*

# Reflection - 1

[8] Armstrong, Karen. *Fields of Blood: Religion and the History of Violence.* New York: Random House LLC. 2014.

[9] Campbell, Joseph. *The Hero of a Thousand Faces.* Princeton New Jersey: Princeton University Press. 1949/1973.

[10] Camus, Albert. *The Myth of Sisyphus and Other Essays. Translated from French by Justin O'Brien. Vintage International Random House. New York. March 1991*

[11] Monod, Jacques. *Chance and Necessity.* Alfred A. Knopf, Inc. New York. 1971.

[12] *Compassion Integrity Training. Life University. Atlanta, Georgia.* https://www.compassionateintegrity.org/ *as of 17 May 2020.*

[13] Monod. Chance and Necessity. 43

[14] Ibid. 16 -17. Some argue that crystals have these properties. It is true that crystalline reproduction, e.g., a hyper saturated salt or sugar crystal solution, leads to a repeating invariant structure and form, examples of inorganic invariance. However, only life forms express autonomous morphogenesis, self-generating critical information from one generation to the next through organic invariance.

[15] Ibid. 45-61. According to Monod, it is the asymmetrically structured catalyst in a stereospecific noncovalent complex relationship with the symmetrically structured substrate that demonstrates a "cognitive" function appearing to contradict the second law of thermodynamics, i.e., positive entropy. For Monod, these phenomena immediately recall Maxwell's demon. In the nineteenth century, physicist James Maxwell conducted a thought experiment. He posited a hypothetical personage sitting at a special gate between two closed chambers filled with any kind of gas. The demon would cognitively "decide" to move the fast-moving particles to one chamber and the slow-moving particles to the other, requiring no energy. He would simply lift the hatch at the right time. This "cognitive function" seemed to defy the second law. It was only later, as Monod explains, that the "riddle" was solved by French physicist Leon Brillouin, based on the earlier work by Leo Szilard (biographical sketch at https://www.jewishvirtuallibrary.org/leo-szilard *site as of Jan 29, 2019). Brillouin*

*demonstrated that "the exercise of the demon's cognitive function, i.e., information, had necessarily to entail the consumption of a certain amount of energy which, on balance, precisely offset the lessening entropy within the system as a whole. To work the hatch 'intelligently,' the demon must first have measured the speed of each particle of gas. Now any reckoning—that is to say, any acquisition of information—presupposes an interaction or movement/action which therefore requires energy consumption." Thus, as is believed today, information is entropy.*

# Reflection – 2

[16] Becker, Ernest. *The Denial of Death.* New York: Simon and Schuster; Free Press Paperbacks. 1973; 255.

[17] Ibid. 101.

[18] Ibid. 68-69.

[19] Ibid.

[20] In the mid-1970s, Becker understood the language of Kierkegaard to be the same as the language of the modern psychology of the time. Kierkegaard's description of the "beast not being qualified by 'spirit'" is read by Becker as "not being qualified by 'self,'" i.e., "spirit" equals "self." Lower animals have no sense of "self" or "spirit" like that of man. In Kierkegaard's description of man as a "synthesis of the (soulish and bodily," Becker reads "soulish" as "self-conscious." Today, many use the term "soul" to mean a person's "intellect and emotions," and the term "spirit" to mean a person's consciousness of self, of other life, and of one's interconnectedness in the cosmos. So, we say that man's nature is a synthesis of "body, soul, and spirit."

[21] Ibid. 142 - 143. According to Becker, we observe this mechanism of transference throughout our development, from childhood onward. Transference can be viewed as the individual's "attempt at creating an environment that will give [him/her] safety and satisfaction… [thus] banishing anxiety from it." We observe this mechanism operant among groups, as well as even nations. Take for example the rise of Nazism and the promise of safety and satisfaction offered by Hitler, as negative as that turned out to be. There are positive examples of group transference, though nonperfect, such as nations that adopt democratic principles. Psychoanalysts understand this transference as "falsifying" the reality of the dread and anxiety [of death]. They saw it as a "regressive phenomenon, uncritical, wishful, a matter of automatic control of one's world." Becker cites several definitions of transference from such notable psychoanalysts as W.V. Silverberg, Erich Fromm, Carl G. Jung, and Alfred Adler. Becker's excerpt of Fromm's definition is most telling: "In order to overcome his sense of inner emptiness and impotence, [man]…chooses an object onto whom he projects all his own human qualities: his love, intelligence, courage, etc. By submitting to this object, he feels in touch with his own qualities; he feels strong, wise, courageous,

*and secure. To lose the object means the danger of losing himself. This mechanism, idolatry or worship of an object, based on the fact of the individual's alienation, is the central dynamism of transference, that which gives transference its strength and intensity."*

[22] *Kierkegaard. The Concept of Dread. Princeton: University Press edition, 1957, translated by Walter Lowrie; 144.*

[23] *Camus, Albert. The Myth of Sisyphus and other Essays. New York and Toronto: Random House, Inc. March 1991 (Orig. 1955).*

[24] *Ibid. 123.*

[25] *Sean Carroll*

[26] *Planck's constant—The Planck constant (denoted h, also called Planck's constant) is a physical constant that is the quantum (unit) of action, central in quantum mechanics.*

# Reflection – 3

[27] Charles E. Curran, American Roman Catholic priest, and moral theologian, currently Elizabeth Scurlock University Professor of Human Values at Southern Methodist University, Dallas, TX.

[28] From open access https://plato.stanford.edu/entries/kant/ on 04 January 2021.

[29] Ibid.

[30] https://www.iep.utm.edu/bentham/ 12 July 2019, author: William Sweet, wsweet@stfx.ca, St. Francis Xavier University, Canada.

[31] Ibid.

[32] https://iep.utm.edu/mill-eth/; author Michael Schefczyk, Michael.schefczyk@kit.edu,Karlsruhe Institut fur Technologie, Germany.

[33] Eisler, Riane. Nurturing our Humanity: How Domination and Partnership Shape Our Brains, Lives, and Future. Oxford University Press. 2019

[34] Curran, Charles E. The Catholic Moral Tradition Today: A Synthesis. Washington DC: Georgetown University Press. 1999.

[35] Niebuhr, H. Richard. The Responsible Self: An Essay in Christian Moral Philosophy. Westminster John Knox Press: Louisville, KY. 1963.

[36] Fletcher, Joseph F. Situation Ethics – The New Morality. Westminster John Knox Press; Louisville, Kentucky. 1966

[37] Taken from http://www.bbc.co.uk/ethics/introduction/situation_1.shtml July 5, 2019.

[38] Ibid.

[39] Curran, The Catholic Moral Tradition Today. 65-66

[40] Ibid.

[41] Ibid. 66-69

[42] *Ibid. 70*

[43] *Ibid*

[44] *Ibid. 71*

# Reflection – 4

[45] *https://en.wiktionary.org/wiki/ontology 19 March 2018.*

[46] *Curran, Charles E. The Catholic Moral Tradition Today: A Synthesis. Washington DC:Georgetown University Press.*

[47] *Refer to Doty, James R. et al editors. The Oxford Handbook of Compassion Science….2017.; and Trezciak, S. and Mazzariah. Compassionomics…. 2019 for current scientific evidence.*

[48] *Personal communication. 2014.*

[49] *Niebuhr, H. Richard. The Responsible Self: An Essay in Christian Moral Philosophy. Louisville,KY: Westminster John Knox Press. [1963]. See also for a general survey of Christian ethics, Beach, Waldo;Niebuhr, H. Richard. Christian Ethics. New York, NY: The Ronald Press Company. [1955].*

[50] *Ibid. 61*

[51] *The Catholic Moral Tradition. 73*

[52] *Ibid. 76 Curran references Schweiker, Responsibility and Christian Ethics, pp.90-130, noting "this contemporary context for a responsibility approach is highlighted."*

[53] *Ibid. 76*

[54] *Quoted words in this sentence from the Charter for Compassion, www.charterforcompassion.org, 2009*

# Reflection – 5

[55] *The medical school requires these reports, called Vital Report Reflections (VRR), as part of a medical student's training during various clinical rotations. The sessions at which VRRs are discussed are usually facilitated by one trained in the field of biomedical ethics.*

[56] *Though permission has been given by the students to reproduce their reports here, their names and locator information have been sanitized. Some of the material is by nature graphic. I have added bracketed information where perhaps clarity is needed for some readers.*

[57] *The scientific literature on empathy defines empathy as the ability to feel and understand the feelings, thoughts, and actions of the other. Empathy consists of two essential components: affective empathy which is the ability to emotionally resonate with the other, and cognitive empathy which is the ability to consider the situation of the other, to step into the shoes of the other in an attempt to understand their feelings, thoughts, and actions. Both components are necessary for true empathy. Psychopaths are well known for their cognitive ability to empathize, but lack emotional resonance, which allows them to do harm without remorse or regret. When an experience or awareness is excessive, overwhelming, or continuously stressful, empathic distress (focus on self rather than focus on the other) results and the relationship suffers. Some mistakenly describe empathic distress as "compassion fatigue," but that terminology is a misnomer. Properly understood, compassion is a motivation to action, not the action (or inaction) itself, which requires wisdom and discernment. See Compassion Integrity Training at: www.compassionateintegrity.org, Skill 7.*

# Reflection - 6

[58] Taken from https://www.psychologytoday.com/us/blog/hide-and-seek/201606/these-are-the-7-typeslove 29 November 2018. As described, these are based on classical writings of Plato and Aristotle and on J.A. Lee's 1973 book Colours of Love.

[59] Tillich, Paul. Morality and Beyond. New York, NY: Harper and Rowe Publishers. 1963. 20

[60] https://www.google.com/search?q=amorality+definition&rlz=1C1GCEU_enUS935US935&oq=amorality+definition&aqs=chrome..69i57.6756j0j15&sourceid=chrome&ie=UTF-8; cited 24 May 2021.

[61] Tillich. Morality and Beyond. 38-39

[62] Ibid. 39

[63] Ibid. 40-41

[64] D-Vasilescu, Elena Ene. Paul Tillich on History and Socialism. Paper presented at Oxford University, January 2000. Resource https://www.researchgate.net/publication/265638623_Paul_Tillich_on_History_and_Socialism April 4, 2019. p 17.

[65] In this paper, the word kairos means "right time," in the theological sense of the end-time presence of the Kingdom of God; and kairoi means periodic interventions of God into the physical world along the arrow of time and space – past, present, and future – interventions not dependent on human creativity, but rather on God breaking through until kairos." The word prophetism changed by me to "prophecy" to avoid falling into the "ism's" category being described by the author in the quoted statement.

[66] Ibid. 82-95

[67] Armstrong, K., Brown-Campbell, J. The international Charter for Compassion was unveiled November 12, 2009, in Washington, DC, viewed around the world, leading to establishment of a worldwide compassion movement. The Charter for Compassion is a U.S. 501(c)(3) tax exempt non-profit organization. To learn more and to affirm the Charter go to www.charterforcompassion.org

[68] *Seppala, Simon-Thomas, Brown, Worline, Cameron and Doty, James R., Editors. The Oxford Handbook of Compassion Science. Oxford Univ Press: New York. 2017*

[69] *Compassion Integrity Training. Life University, Atlanta, Georgia USA; www.compassionateintegrity.org. 2019.*

[70] *Kukk, Kristopher. Verbal communication 2019. Kukk indicates that for very young children, empathy is not a necessary element for compassion. He claims studies show that very young children express compassionate action without there being any element of empathy identified. My thought is that empathy, though genetically determined, matures to obvious expression only as we develop from infancy to toddler, to adolescent, to adult and beyond. The scientific research strongly suggests we are hardwired with empathy for survival purposes. (See multiple studies in The Oxford Handbook of Compassion Science, 2017.*

[71] *Trzeciak, S. and Mazzarelli, A. Compassionomics. Studer Group Publishing: Pensacola FL. 2019. 31 pages of references of references of references. According to research standards this is considered a very complex review of the current literature on compassion studies in healthcare.*

# Reflection - 7

[72] *Mind and Life Conversations with the Dalai Lama, https://youtu.be/AoAEEAq8idU as of January 27, 2020*

[73] *Gobodo-Madikizela, Pumla. A Human Being Died That Night: Forgiving Apartheid's Chief Killer. Portabella Books, LTD: London, UK. 2006.*

[74] *Ibid. 38*

[75] *Ibid. 34*

[76] *https://seelearning.emory.edu/ as of 11/03/2022.*

# Reflection- 8

[77] *Charter for Compassion*

[78] *https://charterforcompassion.org/charter-for-compassion-education-institute*

[79] *ThinkEqual. https://thinkequal.org/*

[80] *SEE Learning. https://seelearning.emory.edu/*

[81] *CCT. https://www.compassioninstitute.com/*

[82] *CBCT. https://www.compassion.emory.edu/*

[83] *CIT. https://www.compassionateintegrity.org/*

[84] *CIT is currently developing two additional skills, 11 and 12, thus increasing Compassion in Systems Series III to four skills. The improved program should be operational early 2024.*

# Epilogue

I began these Reflections with a quote from Paul of Tarsus: "If there is any excellence and if there is anything worthy of praise, think about these things." We have thought and reflected on "these things:" our cosmic and human history, our nature, our morality and ethics, a "new" relationality responsibility ethic, and our need for love and compassion, forgiveness, reconciliation, and restoration in seeking true peace and healing in our world. We have delved into the inner recesses of our body and mind and reached out into the cosmos in search of the most excellent way. And in the process, I hope we have discovered the true nature of our yin/yang, the balance of forces within us, and an important truth about who we are; that is, physical and spiritual beings with the potential for both good and evil. We have a choice. Paul of Tarsus advises us to make this choice:

> *"Live by the Spirit, I say, and do not gratify the desires of the flesh [using the language of today, the physical, mental, and emotional desires, C.O.B] ...the fruit of the Spirit is love, joy, peace, patience, kindness, generosity, faithfulness, gentleness, and self-control. There is no law against such things."—Galatians 5:16,22-23*

It seems obvious to me that to be and become truly the best we can be, we each need to choose—not be compelled—to "live by the Spirit," thereby expressing the fruit of the Spirit and the actions it inspires. This is what compassion-cultivation training does. Such education and training is an internal journey leading to a more resilient spiritual life of goodness, beauty, and truth. This, in turn, leads to compassionate and loving right actions that include forgiveness, reconciliation, and restoration. This process leads to peace and healing.

We, humans, sense a potentially beneficent spiritual dimension in our nature, as well as a potentially malevolent dimension. Perhaps, just perhaps, this multipotential spirituality comes from what theoretical physicists call supersymmetry which suffuses the symmetrical physical reality we know so well. Of course, we cannot see or fully experience supersymmetry. If this is true, then one might ask: "Is this supersymmetry benevolent? Or is it always impartial, like the shining of the sun, nurturing us toward growth and development as described by Paul of Tarsus? Is it the ultimate driving force along the arrow of time guiding us toward the best way as we move closer and closer toward that last rite of passage—death—back into the supersymmetry from which we came?" Interesting to contemplate.

Indeed, may it be so.
And may the Spirit be with you! ☺ LOVE

# Acknowledgments

My soulmate and friend of 54 plus years, Conoly Lemon Barker, without whose constant loving support and encouragement over the years, and especially over the last seven to eight years, this book would not have been completed.

Early Years

My mother, Lucy Jay (Baker) Barker, father Gilbert Harrison Barker, and siblings Ashley, Freddie, Anne, and Warren for their nurturing and friendship during my early formative years and throughout their lifetimes.

My middle school and high school teachers, especially middle school science teacher Ms. Godwin and high school biology teacher Ms. Grady Massey for their gift of the love of science.

My high school buddies Henry Harnage and Harry Davis, good guys, for friendship and camaraderie and for keeping me on the "straight and narrow."

My mentors at our community hospital laboratory Director Ms. Edith Roberts and hospital pathologists Drs. Davis, Stith, and Nelson for their enthusiastic work ethic that inspired me to pursue medical school.

<u>College and Medical School/Practice Years</u>

My college fraternity brothers, many of whom went on to study medicine, for their camaraderie, and especially appreciated the friendship, encouragement, and compassionate support of brother Dr. Gary Broadrick, who was a senior medical student and assisted with my interview when I applied to Emory Medical School.

My medical colleagues in Valdosta, Georgia, especially Drs. Frank Coleman, Joe Stubbs, Tom and Hank Moseley, Jerry Light, and Frank

Smith, all exemplified competent, caring, and compassionate medicine and surgery, along with so many nurses, paramedics, and allied health providers, especially nurse educator Becky Flythe and Gloria Grubb in helping me set up one of the very first American Diabetes Association (ADA) approved Diabetes Education Programs in the United States.

Thanks to my Presbyterian Church (USA) pastor Dwyn Mounger for his loving support and encouragement in outreach and missions in the U.S. and Worldwide, especially my trips to Zaire and Haiti.

## Navy Medicine Career Years

Thank you to colleagues who demonstrated true servant leadership: Jim Devoll, Don Arthur, Andy and Susi Bellenkes, Professor Susan Baker at Johns Hopkins School of Public Health, Dwight Fulton and Faith Burrell, Jerry and Jeannie Patee, "Hoppy" and Judy Hopkins, Nick and Barbara Davenport, Mike Malone, Joan Engel, Bob Matthews, Pat Netzer, and Gayle Pollock.

## Dallas Texas Retirement Years

Thank you to the Dallas Military Evaluation and Processing Station colleagues and staff, especially Ms. Ellsworth, Ms. Jackson, "Virgie" Harding, Ms. Woods, Ms. Tenisha Chism for their support, and Dr. Phan, Dr. Tony Lehner, Dr. Alan Bates, and Dr. April Hurlston for their expert leadership in a very complex system.

Thank you to Wednesday's Men's Christian Fellowship, especially for my friends Boxley Boggs, Bob and Eric VanderDrift, and Leon Wyatt.

My Richardson Texas Saint Barnabas Presbyterian Church (USA) pastors Tom Gibbons, Katy Rigler, and Owen Gray; also Southern Methodist Perkins seminary professors Rebecca Miles, Ruben Habito, Jamie Clark-Soles, and Charlie Curran.

A special thank you to my fellow "Filosophs" who showed such deep thoughtfulness and knowledge in search of truth and who expressed such deep friendship and love over the years – David Alkek, Jack Youngkin, Paul

Tobolowsky, Paul Peterson, Lannie Hughes, Rob Olson, Tom Hampton, David Drumm, and Bennett Litwin. Appreciate the wise counsel of Paul Tobolowsky and Rob Olson with the book manuscript.

A special thank you to past Richardson Mayor Bob Townsend who had great foresight in creating Richardson Interfaith Alliance which introduced me, a Christian, to so many of my current Muslim, Buddhist, Hindi, Baha'i, and Jewish friends who have deepened my spiritual faith journey and understanding of our common humanity and interdependence.

Many thanks and acknowledgment of all those who have journeyed with me with the international Charter for Compassion since its founding in 2009 for its role in fostering true peace and healing through love and compassion, forgiveness, reconciliation, and restoration with the Golden Rule as guiding principle – special thank you to Karen Armstrong, founder, and Joan Brown Campbell, founder and friend, along with Albert (Penny) Pennybacker, Amin Hashwani, Marilyn Turkovich, Gard Jameson, Yaffa Maritz, Laura Burgess, Cristina Gonzalez, Susan Soleil, Ann Helmke, and Ole Kjorrefjord. We have formed a true "Circle of Trust."

A very special thank you to my spiritual friend and guide during these past half dozen years, Caroline Martin, a writer, and author in her own right, who generously blessed me with the Foreword to this book. Thank you, Caroline.

Love and special thanks to my wonderful sister in law, Karene Barker, who with my brother Warren, let me vicariously travel and sight see with them on their RV journeys across the U.S. by way of short videos and clarifying narratives during my terminal illness.

And many thanks to my daughter Emma McDonald and Julie Schelling for their practical advice for self-publishing, to Emma for her help with the audio version of this book, to Sarah Aschenbach for initial editing of the manuscript, and to the Amazon Book Publishing Center team who have worked diligently to publish in a timely fashion, given time constraints and relative urgency. Thank you, Imran Rafi Khan and Gabriella Perez, as project manager, Emma as assistant project manager, and Eman Najam as the editor.

# Bibliography

Armstrong, K., Brown-Campbell, J., Founders. The Charter for Compassion, 2009 @ www.charterforcompassion.org.

Armstrong, Karen. *Fields of Blood: Religion and the History of Violence*. New York: Random House LLC. 2014.

Biblical citations from *New Revised Standard Version*, 1989.

Beach, Waldo; Niebuhr, H. Richard. *Christian Ethics*. New York, Ronald Press, 1955.

Becker, Ernest. *The Denial of Death*. New York, Simon and Schuster, 1973. Kierkegaard. *The Concept of Dread*. Princeton University Press, 1957.

Bentham @ https://www.iep.utm.edu/bentham/ cited 12 July 2019.

Campbell, Joseph. *The Hero of a Thousand Faces*. Princeton New Jersey: Princeton University Press. 1949 / 1973.

Camus, Albert. *The Myth of Sisyphus and Other Essays*. New York, Random House, 1991.

Carroll, Sean M. The Particle At the End of the Universe: How the Hunt for the Higgs Boson Leads Us to the Edge of a New World. New York, Dutton, 2012.

Chalmers, David. 2014 TED Talk "How do you Explain Consciousness." Cited 16 May 2020 @ https://www.ted.com/talks/david_chalmers_how_do_you_explain_consciousness/discussion?langugae=en#t-73764
07 May 2023: https://www.youtube.com/watch?v=uhRhtFFhNzQ

Curran, Charles E. *The Catholic Moral Tradition Today: A Synthesis*. Washington DC: Georgetown University Press. 1999.

Doty, James R. et al. *The Oxford Handbook of Compassion Science*. Oxford University Press, 2017.

D-Vasilescu, E. Paul Tillich on History and Socialism. Oxford University. 2000. Cited @ https://www.researchgate.net/publication/265638623_Paul_Tillich_on_History_and_Socialism April 4, 2019.

Eisler, Riane. Nurturing our Humanity: How Domination and Partnership Shape Our Brains, Lives, and Future. Oxford University Press, 2019.

Fletcher, Joseph F. *Situation Ethics – The New Morality*. Westminster John Knox Press; Louisville, Kentucky, 1966.

Gobodo-Madikizela, P. A Human Being Died That Night: Forgiving Apartheid's Chief Killer. London, UK, Portabella Books, 2006.

Kant @ https://plato.stanford.edu/entries/kant/ cited 04 January 2021.

Karlin, M., Osawa De Silva, B. Compassion Integrity Training. Life University. Atlanta, Georgia
@ https://www.compassionateintegrity.org/ as of 17 May 2020.

Kierkegaard, S. The Concept of Dread. Princeton University Press, 1957.

Mill @ https://iep.utm.edu/mill-eth/ cited 13 July 2019.

Monod, Jacques. Chance and Necessity. Alfred A. Knopf, Inc. New York. 1971.

Niebuhr, H. Richard. The Responsible Self: An Essay in Christian Moral Philosophy. Westminster John Knox Press, Louisville, KY, 1963

Reucroft, S. What Exactly Is the Higgs Boson?" Scientific American. Cited 16 May 2020 @ https://www.scientificamerican.com/article/what-exactly-is-the-higgs/.

Situational Ethics, http://www.bbc.co.uk/ethics/introduction/situation_1.shtml cited July 5, 2019.

Tillich, Paul. Morality and Beyond. New York, Harper and Rowe Publishers, 1963.

The Seven Types of Love. https://www.psychologytoday.com/us/blog/hide-and-seek/201606/these-are-the-7-types-love cited 29 November 2018.

Tobolowsky, Paul. Stardust Dancing: A Seeker's Guide to the Miraculous. Charleston: Create Space, 2013.

Trzeciak, S., Mazzarelli A. Compassionomics: The Revolutionary Scientific Evidence that Caring Makes a Difference, Pensacola Studer Group, 2019.

07 May 2023: https://www.youtube.com/watch?v=uhRhtFFhNzQ

## About the Author

*Charles Barker MD, MPH, Th.M., is founder of Compassionate Dallas/Fort Worth, a non-profit organization that promotes the Charter for Compassion, the value of compassion and compassionate action in the Dallas/Fort Worth metroplex with the Golden Rule as core operating principle. He is currently a member of the international Charter for Compassion, having served as its Chair from 2019 to 2021.*

*Dr Barker's experiences are in the field of medicine, with emphasis in preventive medicine and biomedical ethics. He practiced private solo family medicine for fifteen years, followed by U.S. Navy Aerospace Medicine for 20 years, and for the past 15 years has dedicated his life to theological studies, ethics, and compassion work, focusing on compassion education and training. He lives with his wife Conoly in north Dallas and cherishes his three children and six grandchildren.*

www.ingramcontent.com/pod-product-compliance
Lightning Source LLC
Chambersburg PA
CBHW050255120526
44590CB00016B/2366